Side Piece Is the New Concubine

Reclaiming the Identity, Worth, and Purpose You Lost Along the Way

By Lakisha Shepard

Produced by Ebony Nicole Smith | Ebony Nicole Smith Consulting, LLC | ebonynicolesmith.com

The events and conversations in this book have been set down to the best of the author's ability, although some names and details have been changed to protect the privacy of individuals.

ISBN 979-8-234-07853-7 (paperback)

Unless otherwise noted, all Scripture is from KJV Bible.

First Edition: June 2026

Dedication

This book is first and foremost dedicated to the Lord.
Lord, you were with me when I was broken.
You were with me when I was lost.
You were with me when I didn't fully understand Your plan,
yet You never let go of me.
This book belongs to You.

Table of Contents

A Prayer for the Reader

Father God,

I pray for every reader who opens this book. Prepare her heart to receive truth, correction, healing, and hope. Let these pages minister with compassion and conviction. Let shame be broken, let hidden wounds come into Your light, and let every woman who reads this be reminded that she is deeply loved by You.

Guide her toward freedom. Restore her identity. Strengthen her spirit. Help her hear Your voice above every lie, every counterfeit love, and every place of compromise.

May this book not only be read but received. May it point every reader back to Jesus Christ, the One who heals, restores, and makes whole.

In Jesus' name,

Amen.

Disclaimer

This book is a personal reflection of the author's life experiences, spiritual journey, and the lessons learned along the way. It is intended to inspire, encourage, empower, and bring awareness to real-life situations, but it is not intended to serve as professional advice.

Nothing in this book should be considered a substitute for medical, psychological, legal, or professional counseling. This book is not intended to diagnose, treat, or replace any form of medical care, therapy, or prescribed treatment. Readers are encouraged to seek licensed professionals for any physical, mental, emotional, or legal concerns.

While spiritual principles and personal insights are shared throughout this book, it is not meant to replace a personal relationship with God, pastoral guidance, or wise counsel from trusted spiritual leaders.

Every individual's situation is unique. Therefore, any decisions made based on the content of this book are solely the responsibility of the reader.

By reading this book, you acknowledge that the author is not liable for any outcomes that may arise from the application or misapplication of its content.

Side Piece is the New Concubine

Introduction

Not the "me" I am today. But the me I used to be before God healed me, before my spiritual growth, before understanding what love truly meant. Before God blessed me with my husband, my protector, my covering, my Bishop, before God restored my identity, I lived in that same deception. I lived in that compromise. I lived in that desperate place, As the cliche goes, "I was looking for love in all the wrong places."

I was looking for love in places where love didn't even live.

Let me be real with you.

There was a time when I was that woman who lived in a deceptive world. I was the one answering calls in the middle of the night, pretending I didn't hear the silence on holidays. I was the one who made excuses for why he couldn't stay, why I couldn't post him, why I had to share what should've been sacred. I tried to convince myself that I was strong and in control, but the time I was good and tired, I accepted the idea that this is how love works, and there is no way out.

But the truth is, I was broken; I was mentally exhausted, and my spirit was convicted.

I had mistaken attention for affection. I had mistaken sex for connection. I had mistaken control over confidence. And worse, I had mistaken that man for a blessing when he was really a distraction dressed in potential.

And Lord knows, potential will trap you if you let it.

You'll wait for him to "get it together." You'll hold on, thinking maybe he'll choose you next time. You'll accept less and less while calling it love, when really, it's just emotional starvation. You'll become comfortable in chaos because peace feels foreign. You'll lose years, tears, and parts of yourself just trying to keep someone who was never meant to be kept.

That was my reality.

Until God intervened.

There came a moment, no, a breaking, where I had to confront the truth: I was living beneath the woman I was created to be. I had settled for being a shadow when I was born to walk in the light. I had accepted crumbs from a table I wasn't even supposed to be sitting at. And I had allowed my trauma and my insecurities to convince me that I was only worthy of partial love.

But God.

When God intervened in my life, He revealed the true essence of grace to me. It was at that moment that I began to realize the healing process had started. Slowly, painfully, but beautifully, I began to see myself through His eyes. I started to understand that being chosen isn't about being convenient; it's about being honored. It's not about secrecy;

it's about sacredness. It's not about being someone's backup plan; it's about being God's divine match.

And when I stopped entertaining counterfeit love, I made room for the real thing. I was no longer bound to someone asking me to shrink to feed their ego, but through Christ's Love and the Word of God, I was encouraged to rise with purpose. And now, when I see those same situations play out on my screen, I feel something different.

Gratitude.

Because I don't live there anymore.

I no longer dwell in the house of insecurity, confusion, and compromise. I no longer wait by the phone for someone who doesn't respect my worth. I no longer chase validation in places that only devalue me. I've moved out. I've upgraded. I've been restored.

So, this book? It's not about shame. It's not about blame. It's not even about the man.

It's about us.

It's about every woman who has ever loved too hard, waited too long, cried too often, or settled too deeply. It's about those of us who became sidepieces not because we were weak, but because we were wounded. It's about the spiritual inheritance of concubinage that's been passed down and disguised in different forms, from biblical times to today's DMs and toxic "situationships."

But more than that, this book is about freedom.

It's about truth-telling, healing, and stepping fully into the woman God always intended you to be. My sister, you are not a sidepiece. You are not an afterthought. You are not a temporary thrill. You are a daughter of the King of Kings, the Lord of Lords. You are worth the wait. You are worthy of being chosen, cherished, and covered.

So, if you've ever lived in that house, I want you to know you don't have to stay there anymore.

There is more for you.

Through God there is healing, wholeness, and life after broken love. My All, my everything, will walk you out of that place, just like He did for me.

Chapter One: The History of the Concubine

Before we can talk about the modern-day "side piece," we need to understand her spiritual ancestor: the concubine.

Because long before there were secret situationships, side-chick Saturdays, or Instagram story drama, there were concubines, women who lived in the shadows of powerful men, women who were taken, held, and used, but never truly chosen.

What Is a Concubine?

A concubine was a woman who lived with a man and had a sexual relationship with him, but without the full status or rights of a wife. She could be kept but not covenanted with. She could bear children but not carry the full honor of a household. Her position was legally recognized, but never spiritually elevated.

Concubines existed in many cultures, but the Bible gives us a clear lens on how they were used, abused, and passed down across generations. In ancient Israel and surrounding civilizations, concubinage was seen as a legal but inferior form of union. Men, especially kings and wealthy landowners, had multiple wives and concubines, the wives for political alliance and legacy, the concubines for pleasure, offspring, or household service.

But don't be fooled: no matter what the arrangement is, the concubine was still secondary.

She had limited rights. She couldn't demand loyalty. She didn't hold the inheritance. She was chosen but not fully committed. And most importantly, she was expendable.

- **She was usually chosen for her beauty or availability, not her character.**
- **She did not hold the same authority or honor as a wife.**
- **She was often controlled, not cherished.**
- **She had no guarantee of loyalty or provision.**
- **She could be dismissed at will.**

Biblical Examples of Concubines

Let's be real, there's no better place to understand the spiritual roots of the concubine than in the Word.

Hagar (Genesis 16)

Hagar was Sarah's Egyptian maidservant, given to Abraham to bear a child because Sarah didn't believe she could conceive. Hagar wasn't Abraham's wife. She was a tool used to fulfill a plan born out of doubt. She bore Ishmael, but once Sarah had Isaac, Hagar and her child were cast out.

Even though God saw her and blessed her son, Hagar's story shows us this: You can be used to carry something great, but still be mistreated if you're not walking in your rightful position.

The Levite's Concubine (Judges 19)

One of the most tragic and violent stories in the Bible, this unnamed concubine left her Levite "husband" and was later taken back by him. During their return, she was abused, raped, and ultimately died, while her master remained asleep. He then cut her body into pieces and sent it across Israel as a message of outrage.

Her life and her death were treated as a symbol. Disposable. Voiceless. A warning to us all: when your presence is tolerated but your life is not protected, you are not in a covenant, you are in captivity.

King Solomon's 300 Concubines (1 Kings 11:3)

Solomon had 700 wives and 300 concubines, many of whom were foreign women. These unions weren't just about lust; they were often political, transactional, or culturally influenced. But in the end, they turned Solomon's heart away from God.

This shows us something deep: a relationship rooted in compromise, no matter how glamorous it may look, will eventually pull you away from your purpose.

The Role of the Concubine

The concubine wasn't just a side relationship; she was a symbol of partial access. She had proximity without priority. She could be desired but not dignified. Her body was accepted, but her voice was silenced. She existed to serve, not to reign. And although some concubines bore children and lived in luxury, they still lacked spiritual covering, legal power, and lasting honor.

Concubines were legal, yes. But they were never equal.

- **They had access, but not the authority.**
- **They had intimacy, but not identity.**
- **They had proximity, but not partnership.**

Does any of this sound familiar?

While the culture has changed, the spirit of the concubine remains alive. She just got a new outfit, a new phone, and a new name: Side Piece.

The Spirit of Concubinage Today

Today, the concubine no longer lives in a palace. She lives in someone's phone, someone's DMs, someone's weekend plans. She doesn't call herself a concubine, but she accepts the same terms:

- No title
- No covenant
- No covering
- No commitment

And often, like the women in the Bible, she didn't set out to become a side piece. She didn't even know she was one. At times, life put her there. Trauma put her there. Low self-worth put her there. The manipulation put her there. Many modern women are not thrust into this role by culture or contract; they walk into it through the cracks in their souls.

Let's talk about those cracks.

Some of us became "the other woman" not because someone forced us, but because trauma led us there.

- Abandonment told us that any attention is better than none.
- Rejection taught us that we should take what we can get.
- Childhood wounds whispered that love must be earned, even if we must compete for it.
- Sexual abuse or confusion distorted what intimacy really looks like.

Others walked into that space through selfishness, yes, our own.

Not all sidepiece stories come from a place of brokenness; some come from a place of pride.

- "He chose me even though he's married."
- "At least he comes to me when he really wants peace."
- "His wife doesn't understand him as I do."

These are not words of healing. They are lies wrapped in entitlement. Sometimes the enemy doesn't even have to seduce us; he lets us sit in our own self-interest.

Let's be honest: selfishness isn't always loud or arrogant. Sometimes, it looks like emotional survival. A desperate hunger for significance. A cry from the little girl inside saying, "Choose me. Love me. See me."

But when you feed spiritual hunger with carnal decisions, you'll always walk away empty. Eventually, I had to come to terms with the emptiness I kept trying to ignore.

Spiritual Reflection: The Spirit of Concubinage

The concubine in scripture is a spiritual mirror for women today who:

Settle for partial love.

Accept a counterfeit version of a partnership.

Wait in silence, hoping for elevation.

Trade access for true commitment.

Whether led there by trauma, selfishness, confusion, or loneliness, the root is always the same:

We forgot who we are.

You were not created to be an extra. You were created to be a wife, a helpmeet, purpose-filled daughter of the King.

"But you are a chosen generation, a royal priesthood, a holy nation..." — 1 Peter 2:9

You are chosen, not convenient. You are royal, not recycled. You are holy, not hidden.

Reflection of Chapter One:

The concubine is not just a historical figure; she is a spiritual posture. One that says, "I'll take what I can get, even if it's not God's best."

If you've ever found yourself in the position of the concubine-whether emotionally, sexually, or spiritually-this chapter is not to shame you. It's to wake you up. Because truth doesn't come to condemn, rather, it comes to free.

You don't have to carry that posture any longer. You may have walked in broken, but you can walk out whole. You may have accepted less, but you no longer have to. God never called you to be a concubine. He called you to be a covenant woman. Royal. Covered. Whole. Worthy.

A Prayer To Break Free From The Spirit Of The Concubine

Heavenly Father,

I come before You today not just as a woman, but as Your daughter. I acknowledge the truth that at times, I have accepted less than what You designed for me. Whether through trauma, loneliness, fear, or even my own selfish choices, I stepped into places You never intended for me to dwell. But today, I choose truth. I choose healing. I choose freedom.

Lord, I repent for every time I allowed myself to live beneath my royal identity. I ask for Your mercy and cleansing for every emotional entanglement, every compromise, every silent agreement I made with the lie that I was only good enough to be "the other woman."

Break every soul tie that's been formed through relationships not sealed in covenant. Uproot every lie that told me I had to settle for partial love, temporary affection, or secret attention. Heal every place in me that was driven by rejection, abandonment, or insecurity.

Remind me, O God, that I am more than desirable; I am divinely designed. I am not a concubine. I am not a substitute. I am not an afterthought. I am Your chosen daughter, a royal priesthood, fearfully and wonderfully made, worthy of love, honor, and protection.

I thank You for the grace to start again. I thank You for the power to walk away from what doesn't honor You or me. And I thank You for the promise that I no longer live there. The concubine's house is no longer my home. I now dwell in purpose, in peace, and in covenant with You.

In Jesus' name,
Amen.

Chapter Two: The Modern Side Piece-Culture's New Normal

We used to hide in shame. Now we are posting it online. We used to mourn over infidelity. Now we make it entertainment. We used to fear being the side piece. Now we volunteer for the role. Something has changed.

Today, we live in a culture where the side piece is not only tolerated but celebrated. She's no longer a secret-she's a status symbol. She's confident, proud, and often praised for her boldness. We've glamorized brokenness. We've dressed up in dysfunction, in luxury. And what's worse, some wives and husbands are okay with it.

Dysfunction in Luxury

I want to take this time to explain my own situation when I was involved with a married man. The truth is people around me not only knew about the relationship. Some of them actually praised it. They would smile in our faces, talk about how beautiful we looked together, and even speak about the possibility of us getting married one day.

There were people opposed to it, of course. But more often than not, because this type of relationship had become so normalized, the encouragement outweighed the warnings. Instead of pushing me toward God's truth, some chose to piggyback off my feelings. They saw how deeply I cared for him, and rather than urging me to walk away, they reinforced what I already wanted to believe.

But is it really anyone's responsibility to warn me, especially if they themselves were not walking in the Christian faith?

At that time, I had to realize that many people in my community weren't living by biblical principles, and even if they claimed to believe in God, they didn't practice their faith openly. In fact, faith wasn't often discussed. So realistically, how could I expect someone to warn me about the lifestyle I was living when that same lifestyle had become normal in their eyes?

Looking back now, I can't place the blame on the people around me. We were two consenting adults choosing to live in sin. Those around us didn't correct me because to them, it wasn't wrong; it was simply "life." The sad truth is, when sin becomes the standard, conviction becomes rare.

What I've learned since then is that not everyone has the spiritual eyes to see what's wrong, especially when the world has normalized it. And I can't expect those who aren't walking with God to hold me accountable to God's standards.

At that time, I didn't need people to pat me on the back or to reinforce my emotions. I needed someone with spiritual discernment to speak truth into my life and tell me to get away from that married man! I needed someone to say this to my face, and not behind my back! But even then, I understand now that the responsibility wasn't theirs. It was mine. Because I knew the Word. I knew right from wrong. I had the conviction of the Holy Spirit- I just chose to silence it.

That's why spiritual accountability is so important. The Bible tells us that "iron sharpens iron" (Proverbs 27:17), meaning we need people in our lives who are walking with God, who can correct us in love when we start to stray. But at that point in my life, I had surrounded myself with comfort, not conviction.

As for me, my own feelings made it easy to justify the situation. I told myself that what we had was beautiful. I convinced myself that his marriage was just a "situation", something he didn't want to be in, while I was the one he truly wanted. Each day, I reminded myself: he loves me, he's unhappy there, but he's happy with me.

I walked boldly into a lie. We went places together, we were seen out in public, and yet deep down, my conscience was not at peace. Even in those moments, I knew something wasn't right. He would always make sure that wherever we went, his wife wasn't around. That alone should have been enough to convict me. But because I let my flesh and selfishness lead the way, I continued convincing myself that everything was okay.

The Rise of the Accepted Side Piece

There was a time when being a "mistress" was shameful; when having someone outside your marriage was seen as betrayal. But now, we call it "an open marriage," "an arrangement," or "poly love."

You've seen it.

- Reality shows that celebrate multiple partners.
- Social media influencers who openly share their status as "the one on the side."
- Men and women who knowingly share a spouse and say, "We just want him to be happy."
- Wives who stay silent, saying, "At least he's coming home to me."

The enemy has desensitized us to the point where betrayal is no longer betrayal-it's just "how things are now."

But just because something is normal in culture doesn't mean it's right in the Kingdom.

Modern Marriages That Permit Side Pieces

We are witnessing something tragic:

In today's world, we are witnessing a modern-day tragedy within marriage itself. What God designed to be sacred and holy has now become casual, compromised, and corrupted by the world's standards.

People have become comfortable allowing others into their marriages, physically, emotionally, and spiritually. It has become normal to invite what God calls unholy into what He created to be sacred. We now live in a time where even within marriages, there are arrangements and open relationships that give permission for what used to be called adultery.

It seems like in this modern day, we see people creating rules, agreements, and so-called "understandings" to justify sin, swinging, open marriages, and relationships built on shared infidelity. Many are ignorant of what sin is and are walking unthinkingly. What used to be considered shameful is now celebrated. What once brought conviction now brings applause.

It grieves my spirit to see how easily the enemy has blinded so many into believing that this is acceptable. Society has turned what God created- a covenant between one man and one woman- into a social experiment that fits the desires of the flesh instead of the design of the Father.

It's like the days of Sodom and Gomorrah all over again. Everything is permissible, and nothing is sacred. The spirit of compromise has invaded homes, pulpits, and marriages. The world calls it freedom, but in God's eyes, it's bondage, it's wicked, and people who are engaging in it become a stench to His nostrils (Isaiah 65:5).

And yet, we must remember that none of this is new to God. The Bible warned us of this time. Just as in the days of Noah, and just as in the days of Sodom, people would live as if there were no consequences until judgment came.

God's design for marriage has never changed. It remains a sacred covenant, not a contract to be negotiated, not a playground for lust, not a partnership of convenience, but a divine reflection of Christ's love for His church.

Scripture Reflection:

"Marriage is honourable in all, and the bed undefiled: but whoremongers and adulterers God will judge."
— Hebrews 13:4 (KJV)

"As it was in the days of Lot; they did eat, they drank, they

bought, they sold, they planted, they builded... Even thus shall it be in the day when the Son of man is revealed."

—Luke 17:28, 30 (KJV)

Reflection Thought:

What the world normalizes, God still condemns. Holiness in marriage is not outdated; it is a divine order.

Marriages That Are Legally Formed but Spiritually Broken.

Some women wear the ring, sign the license, say the vows, but behind closed doors, they've learned to share. They've been conditioned to believe that some love is better than none. That keeping the peace is more important than keeping the promise.

And some husbands justify it by quoting the Bible out of context. "Didn't Solomon have concubines?" "David had multiple wives."

But let's be clear-just because it's recorded in Scripture doesn't mean God approves it. The Bible is a historical book, yes, but it is also a spiritual blueprint. It shows us both the victories of man and the consequences of disobedience.

What The Word Really Says

Genesis 2:24 (KJV) "Therefore shall a man leave his father and his mother, and shall cleave unto his wife: and they shall be one flesh."

One flesh. Not three. Not a rotation. Not a weekend option. One.

This was the first divine covenant between Adam and Eve. Before there was law, before there were nations, before there were cultures, there was marriage. God didn't give Adam options. He gave him Eve. Not Eve and her sister. Not Eve and a standby. Just Eve.

Cleave means to cling tightly, to be joined together inseparably. You cannot cleave to one woman while also creeping with another. It doesn't work that way. God didn't call a man to scatter himself; He called him to commit.

Ephesians 5:25 (NIV) "Husbands, love your wives, just as Christ loved the church and gave himself up for her."

God is not passive about marriage. He doesn't shrug it off as culture does. He holds men accountable for how they treat their wives. He hears the cries of the women who are betrayed. He reminds husbands: "I saw you make that vow. I was there."

And to those who invite others into their marriage, whether for pleasure, arrangement, or pride. God is not mocked. Marriage is a spiritual covenant, not a carnal contract.

Marriage is sacred to God. It is not just a covenant between two people, but a divine institution that He Himself honors, establishes, and protects. Throughout Scripture, God elevates the significance of marriage by using it as one of the most powerful spiritual metaphors we have: Jesus Christ as the Groom, and the Church as His Bride. This comparison is not casual; it is intentional. It reveals just how deeply God values the union of marriage. The same way Christ will one day return for His Bride, pure and prepared, is the same way God expects us to honor, protect, and uphold the covenant of marriage. When we understand that marriage mirrors the relationship between Jesus and the Church, we begin to see how holy, weighty, and sacred that union truly is in the eyes of God.

Hebrews 13:4 (NIV) "Marriage should be honored by all, and the marriage bed kept pure, for God will judge the adulterer and all the sexually immoral."

Read that again: God will judge.

Not Twitter. Not your followers. Not your friends who say, "Girl, do what makes you happy."

God. Will. Judge.

Adultery is still sin. Infidelity is still sinful. Open marriages are still outside of God's original design. There is no filter, no finesse, and no fame that can erase what the Word clearly states.

The Real Cost of the Side Piece Spirit

What the world calls freedom, God calls bondage.

What the world calls open, God calls unfaithful.

And what the world calls modern love, God sees as a return to spiritual slavery, because every time we ignore His blueprint, we return to the chaos He delivered us from.

Romans 6:23 "For the wages of sin is death..."

It might not be physical death, but it can be the death of:

- Trust.
- Covenant.
- Peace in the home.

- Intimacy between spouses.
- Legacy for your children.

What starts as "a little arrangement" becomes spiritual contamination. You can't share what was meant to be sacred and expect to be whole.

I can't really say when I accepted the role of being a side piece, because in truth, I never consciously accepted it. What happened was a process. It wasn't a moment where I made a decision and said, "Yes, I'll be a side piece." Instead, it was a gradual journey that I allowed myself to go through subconsciously because I wasn't thinking. I was just going with the flow. I was allowing my flesh to lead me, because my spirit was already sick and dehydrated from lack of spiritual food and lack of the water of life.

The relationship started with casual conversation, which turned into interest. That interest turned into long phone calls-one or two hours at a time. By then, I had already crossed the line mentally, because I began to open myself up and grow attached. I was vulnerable, and I kept walking into the relationship further and further.

One day, we shared a kiss. That kiss led to a date. That date led to intimacy. And after intimacy, I was there, emotionally, physically, and spiritually entangled. At that time, I didn't even see myself as a side piece. I told myself that what we had was real, but in reality, I had blinded myself, convincing my mind and my flesh that it was love.

The moment I realized how deep I had come when I thought to myself that if I could somehow get his wife's permission to "share" him, maybe the relationship wouldn't feel as sinful.

That thought alone showed how far I had fallen, how consumed I was by my emotions and my flesh.

And all the while, I was still in church. I was ushering. I was praise dancing. I was tithing. I was active. On the outside, I looked like a woman of God. But inside, I was living a double life. I wasn't feeding my spirit; I was feeding my flesh. My flesh was strong, but my spirit was gasping for air.

Here's what feeding the flesh actually looked like for me: I listened to secular music filled with messages of lust, songs glorifying premarital sex, and teaching provocative ways to lure a man physically and sexually. I watched movies that displayed intimacy outside of marriage, with language and images that planted ideas of fornication in my mind. I allowed small "innocent" conversations to become sexual conversations, talking about things that only a husband and wife should share.

I went to church on Sunday but went to secular parties on Friday night. At those parties there was drinking, smoking, dancing, gyrating. I was never a heavy drinker, but I'd find myself taking a drink, or even half a drink, knowing that wasn't even me, that wasn't who I really was. But I stayed in that environment. I surrounded myself with a community that did not serve my spiritual life and did not preserve it.

Feeding my flesh with all of these things opened me up to even more compromise. Other unclean spirits attached themselves to me. Not only was I involved as a side piece, but being in that role connected me to other sins. Because when you're living in sin, that sin will often lead to another sin. Sin has cousins. One compromise invites the next. And if you don't cut it off, they travel together and chain themselves to your soul.

Reflection of Chapter Two:

God's standard for marriage has not changed, even if the culture has.

A man is to leave his father and mother, and cleave to his wife, not his wife and his side piece. God honors one-flesh unions, not open relationships. He blesses faithfulness, not "arrangements." You cannot ask God to bless your marriage while you participate in its destruction.

And to the wives who have accepted it: God sees your tears. But He also wants to restore your voice. You were not created to be quiet in compromise. You were created to be covered in covenant.

Chapter Two Prayer: A Prayer for Restoration of Covenant and Truth

Heavenly Father,

You are the author of love and the designer of marriage. Today, I come before You acknowledging the ways culture has tried to distort what You created to be sacred. Lord, forgive me for the times I accepted or entertained anything less than covenant. Forgive me if I, knowingly or unknowingly, walked in the spirit of the side piece or tolerated it in my life.

Heal my heart, Lord. Heal every place that normalized betrayal. Remove every seed that made me believe that unfaithfulness is okay, as long as it doesn't hurt too bad. I reject the lies of culture, and I receive the truth of Your Word.

I pray for every marriage that is under attack. I pray for wives who have been silenced, and for husbands who have been seduced by the spirit of compromise. Lord, call them back to covenant. Let Your Spirit convict, correct, and restore.

Thank You that I was made for more than being someone's second option. I was made for sacred love. I was made for one-flesh partnership. I was made for divine covenant. I surrender my views of relationships to align with Yours. And I declare: my heart, my body, and my love are sacred.

In Jesus' name,
Amen

Chapter Three: Just a Piece - When Wholeness is Broken by Casual Intimacy

They say, "At least I'm not a side piece." And maybe they're not.

They don't chase someone's husband. They're not sneaking around. There's no "main" woman to compete with. It's just two consenting adults, doing what grown people do, right?

Wrong.

Because while you may not be a side piece, you may still be just a piece.

And in God's eyes, that's still not wholeness.

I want to share my experiences, as this isn't theory- it is my life. There were several times when I found myself having sexual intercourse with an individual who I found extremely attractive, or who found me attractive. One thing would lead to another and, boom, before I knew it, we were in a "relationship."

But these types of relationships were really like playing Russian Roulette. Just because I was sexually active with someone didn't mean they were faithful to me. I may have been loyal and faithful to my partner at the time, but on several occasions, my partner was not faithful to me.

Every time I gave up myself sexually, I wasn't just giving my body; I was giving my time, energy, trust, precious moments. And when I would find out the person had cheated on me, the pain was almost like death. It hurt so deeply because it wasn't just physical; we had become spiritually and emotionally tied. In God's eyes, two had become one. But we had become "one" in an illegal way, like illegal aliens trespassing- connected outside of the covenant, which left me out of alignment with everything I believed.

The world teaches you how to cover the physical elements of your body. It tells you about condoms, birth control, pills, Plan B, and all the ways to prevent pregnancy or protect from STDs. But the world doesn't give you anything to protect your spirit, your mind, or your emotions. While my body was "covered," my spirit was uncovered and vulnerable to spiritual diseases: rejection, insecurity, comparison, jealousy, and envy.

I noticed a pattern. At first, I'd be the apple of his eye. The spark would be strong, but then the fizzle would fade. His attention would drift to another woman, and because my spirit was empty and wounded, I'd find myself attaching to someone else who gave me the attention I wasn't getting anymore. Then the cycle would repeat: spark, intimacy, fizzle, pain, then move on.

With every encounter, I wasn't just giving away pieces of myself; I was also collecting pieces of them, their hurts, their habits, their spirits. My body, my mind, and my soul were never designed for that kind of exchange. Without a covenant, intimacy diminishes you. It leaves you fragmented instead of whole.

The Spirit of Fragmentation

When you give your body to someone outside of God's covenant of marriage, you don't just give them physical access; you split your soul.

You move from being a whole woman, covered, protected, and walking in purpose, to becoming a piece of your former self.

- A piece of your confidence.
- A piece of your identity.
- A piece of your worth.
- A piece of your destiny.

The Bible doesn't treat sex as a casual act; it treats it as a spiritual covenant. Something sacred. Binding. Life altering. Something that joins two people together, not just physically, but spiritually.

1 Corinthians 6:16 (NLT) "And don't you realize that if a man joins himself to a prostitute, he becomes one body with her? For the Scriptures say, 'The two are united into one.'"

That's not just poetry. That's the principle.

Every time you lie down with someone, you take on a piece of them, and you leave a piece of yourself behind. You walk away spiritually lighter, but not in a good way. You begin to live fragmented, while calling it freedom.

When Casual Becomes Costly

We tell ourselves, “It’s just sex.”

But sex outside of covenant is never just sex. It’s an exchange.

You give your body in moments of passion, and what you receive in return is often:

- Confusion
- Soul ties
- Emotional dependence
- Shame
- Guilt
- Delayed destiny

You become a collector of memories that were never supposed to be made. Your spirit becomes a scrapbook of every place you’ve been and everyone you’ve been with. Your body remembers what your spirit regrets. And slowly, piece by piece, your wholeness erodes. When we give ourselves to multiple partners, we don’t just encounter a black book. We become one, carrying names, memories, and spiritual imprints that were never meant to be collected that way.

You’re not a side piece, but you’re still not whole.

You Weren’t Created for Pieces-You Were Created for Covenant

God never designed you to be divided. He didn’t create your body to be a recreational tool. He created it to be a temple, a sacred place reserved for covenant love.

1 Corinthians 6:19–20 (ESV) “Do you not know that your body is a temple of the Holy Spirit within you, whom you have from

God? You are not your own, for you were bought with a price. So glorify God in your body."

That scripture doesn't just apply to "church girls." It applies to every daughter of God who was bought with the blood of Christ.

You are not your own.

You don't belong to lust. You don't belong in late-night texts. You don't belong to someone who hasn't made you a wife. You belong to God. And until your body is given in covenant, it should remain consecrated.

Soul Ties: When Peace Becomes Pieces

When you're intimate with someone, you do more than lie down; you tie up your soul.

Genesis 2:24 (KJV) "And they shall be one flesh."

God said this in the context of marriage, not casual connection. One flesh means complete unity-emotionally, spiritually, and physically. But outside of marriage, that unity becomes a trap. It forms a tie that doesn't have the structure to sustain it.

What happens?

- You can't stop thinking about them.
- You feel emotionally attached after one night.
- You stay longer than you should, even when you're not respected.
- You confuse sexual chemistry with spiritual compatibility.

These are signs that your pieces are scattered. And the more you give yourself without covenant, the more broken your sense of self becomes.

The Enemy's Plan: Divide and Conquer

Satan isn't just after your body-he's after your wholeness.

If he can't turn you into a side piece, he'll settle for turning you into just a piece-scattered, insecure, fragmented, and spiritually numb.

During the time that I was a side piece, I was all of those things.

I was *scattered*; my mind was all over the place, constantly wondering what I could do to keep the spark alive in this man's eyes for me.

I was *insecure*; even though I knew I was a mistress, I still found myself comparing. I would ask myself, "What does his wife have that I don't have? Why is he still there with her if he says he wants to be with me?" That insecurity ate away at me.

I was *spiritually numb*; I didn't feel anything other than what I wanted to feel. I stopped being sensitive to God's Spirit. I stopped being convicted. Instead, I ran after the temporary comfort of his words and his touch.

And I was *selfish*; brokenness made me selfish. I wanted him, and I didn't care what he was connected to. I convinced myself that he wasn't supposed to be with her; he was supposed to be with me. That lie hardened my heart to God's truth, and I gravitated toward all the wrong.

Even when I was not in the role of a side piece but just "a piece," I carried those same struggles. My mind was scattered. I worried about my appearance-was I too small, too petite, not enough? I wanted to keep the attention of whoever I was with. I wanted that sparkle in their eye to stay fixed on me so they would always want me.

In reality, I recognized that I was broken because of compromises I made, and because I accepted things that were contrary to God's Word. I forgot who I am and who God said I am.

I wanted to be loved, and because of that desire, I was willing to compromise my place in God to feel love from another human being. But that "love" was counterfeit. It cost me pieces of myself, and it pulled me further from my true purpose.

Because a fragmented woman is:

- Easier to manipulate
- Slower to walk in purpose
- Quieter in spiritual authority
- Distracted from her calling

The devil doesn't always have to destroy you, sometimes all he has to do is divide you.

A Divine Wake-Up Call Through Chaos

There came a time when everything around me started to unravel. The relationship that once felt so sweet began to reveal its true side-chaotic, unsafe, and unstable. There I was, in an adulterous relationship for two years, waiting for full commitment, and promises made to me, to be kept. What I once thought was love, was lust, dressed up and disguised as love. It was as if God Himself allowed the chaos to rise so that I could finally see clearly.

The more God exposed things to me I began to understand the situation I was in wasn't just emotionally damaging-it had become physically dangerous. The consequences of my choices became painfully real. What had once seemed like a private situation suddenly turned into something much larger.

One night, a series of events unfolded that could have easily ended in tragedy. I found myself in a situation where violence erupted, and in the chaos that followed, lives were put in danger, including my own.

In the midst of that moment, I realized how close I had come to losing everything. I could have lost my life. What had once been a private struggle had suddenly become public.

God used that moment to open my eyes. What looked like a disaster was really divine intervention. He allowed everything to become uncomfortable so that I could no longer stay blind to the truth.

Sometimes God will shake up your world to save your soul. That chaos became my first wake-up call. It was the beginning of my realization that I was living in something that could literally destroy me. God didn't send the danger, but He used it to pull me back toward Him.

Even then, I didn't fully let go. I tried to end things, but the enemy lured me back in. Yet even in my relapse, I could no longer pretend I didn't know better. God had opened my eyes, and once you see truth, you can't unsee it.

The Deeper Realization

Looking back, I can see now just how complicated and sinful my situation truly was. At that time, I was separated but not divorced. I had my own place, my own life, and I convinced myself that being separated meant I was free. But in God's eyes, I wasn't. I was still bound by a marriage covenant that had not been lawfully or spiritually dissolved.

That made what I was doing even more serious. Not only was I a side piece, but I was a side piece living in adultery. And the truth is, I wasn't just connected to a man who was in sin; I was also leading him deeper into sin. It was messy. It was painful. And it was wrong.

But even in that, God showed me mercy. He didn't expose me to destroy me. He exposed me to deliver me. He allowed the chaos in my life to show me what I was really a part of, and He used that truth to begin freeing me. That was the start of my awakening, my moment of clarity-the moment the veil began to lift, and the woman inside me started to see herself through God's eyes for the first time.

Truth: Sometimes God allows the chaos to expose the counterfeit, not to break you, but to free you.

When Truth Found Me

I didn't go looking for exposure-exposure found me. When God decides it's time to bring something into the light, He does it in His own way and in His own timing.

One night, long after I had gone to bed, I couldn't sleep. I kept tossing and turning, my spirit was unsettled. Then I noticed a message on my phone. It was late, and when I looked down at my phone, that's when I saw her name- It was his wife.

My heart didn't drop; instead, I was in awe. It was as if everything around me went still, and I immediately recognized that this was God at work. I remembered the prayer I had whispered to God during my struggle: "Lord, I won't reach out to her, but if You allow her to contact me, I'll tell the truth." And here it was-God literally answering that prayer before my eyes.

She was calm. I didn't sense any anger through her text message. She simply said she had found out and wanted to talk. When she asked if it was okay to call me, I paused, whispered a prayer for strength, and said "Yes, you can call."

When the phone rang moments later, I felt the peace of God come over me. She told me she had found the messages between him and me, and she wasn't calling to fight; she wanted honesty. That's when I knew this was my moment to make things right, not for my reputation, but for my soul.

I told her the truth. I apologized sincerely for the pain I caused and asked her to forgive me. And by God's grace, she did, or at least she said she did.

That conversation didn't end the situation right away, but it did begin my freedom. I felt a weight lifted that night, not because the mess was over, but because I had obeyed God and spoken truth. What the enemy meant for my shame, God used for my shaping. That late-night exchange wasn't by coincidence; it was God's divine timing, reminding me that He always keeps His word.

The House Phone Relapse

Even though I thought that moment was the end of it, it turned out to be just the beginning of my awakening. I changed my cellphone number, thinking that by doing so, I had closed the chapter completely. I thought that new number would be my clean slate, my proof that I had walked away for good.

But I forgot about the house phone.

It sounds small, but that's how the enemy works-through the smallest cracks we overlook. I figured, "He doesn't have my cell number anymore, so I'm free." But one day, when the house phone rang, I looked down and saw a familiar number. Without thinking, my flesh picked up the receiver.

The sound of his voice was all it took. He started saying all the right words, the same words that had kept me bound before. The "I love you's," the "I miss you's," the "you'll always be special to me." I had heard them all before, but because I was still weak in that area, my emotions remembered what my spirit had already been trying to forget.

That's when I learned that true deliverance isn't just cutting someone off-it's closing every open door the enemy can use to get back in. I thought I had shut the door, but I left the latch unlocked. And when temptation knocked, I opened it.

Looking back now, I realize that moment was part of my spiritual training. God was teaching me that deliverance and discipline go hand in hand. He allowed me to see how easy it was to fall when I relied on my own strength instead of His. It was a painful lesson, but a necessary one. Because once I truly surrendered that area to God, the enemy lost his foothold for good.

When The Fall Became The Turning Point

Can you believe I fell back into the same old trap, with the same person? It wasn't just a small stumble; it was a hard fall-on-my-face fall! I had left a crack open, and the enemy crawled right through it. This time, it felt heavier, deeper, and darker than before.

I knew what I was doing was wrong, yet I convinced myself that things might be different now. He told me that he and his wife were separated, that their marriage was over, that there were no more him and her. And because I wanted to believe it, I did. I let those words become truth in my mind, even though I knew better deep down.

Looking back, I can admit that even after knowing better, I allowed myself to be deceived. I let him convince me that their relationship was finished, that I had every right to feel the way I did about him because they were supposedly no longer together. I accepted the deception because it comforted my emotions. But deception always comes with a cost, and this time the cost was clarity.

Before this, his wife and I had spoken a couple of times. Our conversations weren't hostile. We talked about relationships, about pain, and about trying to understand the brokenness that comes with betrayal. I didn't realize it then, but the confusion I felt from those talks was conviction trying to reach me. I was torn between guilt and comfort, between knowing what was wrong and wanting to feel wanted.

And then came the breaking point.

One day, I asked him, "*Where do I stand?*" His response would become the answer that set me free. He told me that he and his wife had decided to work things out, to rebuild and restore whatever they still had together.

But even after saying that, he still wanted to maintain his relationship with me. He told me that he loved me, that he was in love with me, and that he still wanted access to my life. In his mind, he could have both- the marriage and me- and still make it all make sense.

That was the moment my eyes were completely opened. I realized that he wanted to have his cake and eat it too, and that I had been allowing him to do just that. He wanted to keep me in his comfort zone while publicly maintaining his marriage. That realization broke me, but it also freed me.

Because in that instant, my mind went to his wife. If she had decided to work things out with him, it meant she expected to rebuild trust and start fresh. And I couldn't be the reason for her pain anymore. I couldn't keep hurting her, and I couldn't keep hurting myself.

Even after that conversation, there was still a process of letting go. I had already cut the physical ties, but we would still talk now and then. The conversations were brief and harmless on the surface, but they were still open doors to something I no longer wanted. I think part of me wanted him to figure it out, to realize that it was truly over between us.

But over time, through prayer, God gave me the courage and strength to close that door completely. No attachments. No "just friends." No late-night calls. Nothing. I had to cut it off at the root, not just at the surface.

And that's when it finally clicked. I realized that I didn't want to risk losing my future, the promises and blessings that God had already spoken over my life. I couldn't let him ruin what God had already prepared for me.

So, I walked away, for good.

No looking back. No guilt, or shame. Just peace.

And I'm so grateful that I did. Because when I finally let go of what wasn't meant for me, God released what was.

There's Good News: God Can Make You Whole Again

Joel 2:25 (NKJV) "So I will restore to you the years that the swarming locust has eaten..."

Even if you've given yourself away. Even if your soul feels tied in knots. Even if you feel like nothing's left but pieces...

God can restore your wholeness.

He can untie every soul tie.

He can wipe away the shame.

He can renew your mind.

He can heal your body.

He can gather every scattered piece and make you whole again in Him.

I believe this because He did it for me.

It wasn't easy for me to get out of what I was in. I had invested so much time, so many tears, laughter, memories, so many ungodly things that felt so satisfying to my flesh. Walking away wasn't simple. But one day, I realized that if I didn't get out of the relationship I was in, I would always be a side piece. I would never be whole. I would never become the woman God intended me to be.

The wake-up call came like a light bulb turning on. It was as if I could hear him-not only with words but with actions-telling me that I would always be his side piece. His behavior confirmed it. The late nights of intimacy followed by waking up alone in the morning, the repetitive, shallow phone calls, the constant cycle, sooner or later, everything suddenly became clear.

I believe it was the Lord's grace and mercy that lifted the veil off my eyes. He removed the scales from my spiritual vision and allowed me to see the situation for what it truly was. When that happened, I had no choice but to repent. I cried out to God, asking Him to forgive me, to cleanse me, to take away the desires that kept pulling me back into sin.

And God heard me. He knew the sincerity of my heart. He knew my desire not just to be loved, but to be the kind of wife who honors Him, to love someone who first loves the Lord, because if he loves the Lord, I know he'll love me.

It was like spiritual cataracts had been removed from my eyes. Suddenly, I had 20/20 vision in my spirit. I could see clearly what I had been blind to for so long. And when I said yes, a sincere yes, to His will and His way, He began to reveal my brokenness, my true identity, and His deep love for me. By saying yes, I opened the door for God to cleanse me, restore me, and realign me with His purpose.

Reflection of Chapter Three:

There's something powerful about total surrender. When you finally release what God never meant for you, He fills your hands with what was always yours to have: peace, purpose, and His presence.

"It is for freedom that Christ has set us free. Stand firm, then, and do not let yourselves be burdened again by a yoke of slavery." — Galatians 5:1 (NIV)

You may not be a side piece, but if you give yourself away outside of the covenant, you are still at risk of becoming just a piece. Casual sex leads to spiritual fragmentation. You were not made for pieces. You were made for a covenant. Wholeness. Sacred love.

Don't settle for becoming someone's moment. Wait on God to send you someone worthy of being your lifetime.

Chapter Three Prayer: A Prayer for Wholeness After Sexual Fragmentation

Father, in the name of Jesus, I come before You humbly and honestly. There are times I've given my body away without understanding the weight of what I was releasing. I confess that I've allowed myself to become a piece when You created me to be whole. I've lain down in places that didn't honor me. I've shared myself with people who weren't my covenant. And I've carried the weight of those choices in silence.

But Lord, I thank You for being the God who restores—the God who sees my pieces and knows how to put them back together. I ask You now to break every soul tie, every lingering connection, every spiritual residue that is not of You. I release the guilt, the shame, and the lies I've believed. And I receive Your healing.

Make me whole again, God. Let me walk in purity, not just in action, but in identity. Teach me how to protect my body, guard my heart, and wait for Your timing. I am not just a piece. I am a whole woman. I am Yours.

In Jesus' name,
Amen.

Chapter Four: The Wages of Sin-When the Pieces Add Up to Death

Let's not sugarcoat it. Let's not dress it up in grace and ignore the truth. Let's not pretend that God is so loving that He stopped being just.

Let's say it plainly:

"For the wages of sin are death..."— Romans 6:23a (KJV)

That's the Word. That's not my opinion. That's not tradition. That's not church folk talking. That's the Bible.

I was basically a walking corpse. I was alive in the flesh but dead in the spirit. I wasn't living to my full potential in God, because sin had a hold on me. I wasn't living right, and even though my body moved, my spirit was lifeless.

I was walking around as a Christian by name, but not in full obedience. I prayed, I went to church, I ushered, I praise-danced, I lifted my hands, but the part of my life where I allowed myself to live in sin, to be a side piece, canceled out the fullness of my worship. My life had become vain because I was divided. I wasn't living completely for God.

The Bible calls that being lukewarm. And Revelation 3:15–16 says, *"I know your works, that you are neither cold nor hot. I wish you were cold or hot. So then, because you are lukewarm, and neither cold nor hot, I will spew you out of My mouth."*

That was me, lukewarm, straddling the fence between the world and the Word. I was spiritual, ushering and praise dancing one moment and fornicating/committing adultery the next. I lived a double life, thinking I could balance both. But there's no balance walking in sin. it tilts you completely away from God.

I was in a dangerous position, because I was allowing myself to indulge in my desires to act outside of God's will. I was satisfying my desire to have sex with a married man. I was living what my Christian faith called, a lukewarm life. The Book of Revelation 3:15-16 warns believers who are lukewarm. If it hadn't been for God's grace and mercy, I could have died in that sin. I could have opened my eyes in hell because I chose rebellion over repentance. And the hardest truth to admit was that I knew what I was doing was wrong. I just thought that because it was me, somehow it was okay.

It wasn't.

Sin had numbed me, causing me to become selfish, rebellious, and conceited in my thinking. I was alive on the outside but spiritually dead on the inside, a walking corpse, moving through life without life inside of me. But God, by His grace, called those dead bones to live again.

Sin Comes with a Cost

We live in a culture that's gotten comfortable with sin, especially sexual sin.

We tell ourselves:

- "God knows my heart."
- "At least I'm not as bad as so-and-so."
- "We're grown, and we love each other."
- "Everybody does it."
- "We're getting married anyway."

But God is not grading us on a curve. He's measuring us with His Word.

Sin is not a phase.

Sin is not a vibe.

Sin is not a lifestyle.

Sin is death.

And the wages, payment, and result of living in sin leads you to separation from God, both in this life and in the life to come.

Isaiah 59:2 (NIV) "But your iniquities have separated you from your God; your sins have hidden his face from you, so that he will not hear."

You cannot live in willful sin and in return expect full communion with God. You cannot be someone's side piece or just a piece, live in adultery or fornication, and expect to walk in kingdom authority.

Take Bathsheba, for example (2 Samuel 11). Scripture tells us that while her husband Uriah was away at war, she was bathing on the rooftop when King David saw her (2 Samuel 11:2). David desired her, and because he was king, he sent for her. But Bathsheba was not an innocent bystander. She was married, and when she lay with David, she stepped into adultery.

From Bathsheba's perspective, she allowed herself to fall into David's arms. Maybe she felt powerless under the king's command. Maybe she reasoned that it was just one night. Maybe she convinced herself it would stay hidden. But whatever her reasoning, she crossed a line. And that one sin did not stand alone; it birthed another.

When Bathsheba became pregnant, David devised a plan to cover up the sin. First, he tried to bring Uriah home from battle so that Uriah would sleep with her, but Uriah was too loyal to his men and refused (2 Samuel 11:8–11). So, David sent Uriah back to the battlefield with sealed orders that placed him in the front lines where death was certain (2 Samuel 11:15). And Uriah died.

Bathsheba lost her husband. She lost the security of her marriage. She lost the covering of her covenant. All because of one choice to enter into an ungodly union. And even though she later became David's wife, the child conceived from that union died (2 Samuel 12:18). She experienced devastating loss-her marriage, her husband, her child.

And David himself? He bore the weight of his choices. The sword never departed from his house (2 Samuel 12:10). The very thing he sowed in secret grew into a harvest of pain. His sons later struggled with lust, rebellion, and violence, proof that the seed of one sin can ripple down into generations.

But from Bathsheba's side, it is a sober warning. She entered into the arms of another man, knowing she was bound to Uriah, and it set in motion a chain of events she could not control. One sin demanded another sin to cover it. A stolen night of passion led to death, grief, and consequences that could not be erased.

Adultery always takes more than it gives. It promises intimacy but delivers destruction. It promises love but brings loss. It promises secrecy but exposes shame.

And I know that to be true because of what the affair cost me.

In addition to losing myself, I lost the ability to be a true witness for God. I lost the strength of a fully committed relationship with Him. I lost the ability to stand boldly for what was righteous because I was living in sin. I couldn't minister the way my spirit longed to, because I had lost so much strength spiritually by being a side piece.

I could never give the fullness of God's love, His grace, and His mercy, because deep down I knew I was taking advantage of the very grace and mercy He had extended to me. Even while I faithfully attended church, listened to the Word on Sundays, and tried to operate in the gifts He gave me, the anointing wasn't there. My work for God became vain, more carnal than spiritual, because I was knowingly living in sin. It made me a hypocrite, and it dulled the effectiveness of my witness.

Sin cost me my character. Though I was naturally kind, loving, and gentle toward others, that sin dimmed the light of God inside me- almost snuffed it out. The shame of it weighed on me. I have always been private about my personal life, but in that situation, I couldn't hide. Being a side piece wasn't a secret. It exposed me. It exposed my vulnerability. It exposed my shame.

I lost precious years that could have been spent letting God use me fully. I lost opportunities to testify of His love, because how could I tell someone to walk in holiness when I was\ not living rightly? I lost my peace and joy. I was constantly on edge, wondering if I would ever escape that situation.

We see it often on the news or on reality shows: love affairs leading to violence, marriages torn apart, situations ending in tragedy. Well, that could have been me. I could have died while right in my foolish lifestyle and opened my eyes in hell.

The most dangerous place for a Christian is believing you're still safe under grace while you're willfully living in sin. I didn't realize at the time that God could have removed His hedge of protection from me at any moment. But He didn't. And I'm grateful.

Yes, I have experienced significant losses. However, through these losses, God has remade me. He has restructured and restored me into something greater than I have ever been. Now, even my brokenness serves as a tool, allowing my testimony to witness, as I share it in this book.

Death Doesn't Always Come in a Casket

The wages of sin aren't just about your heart stopping; it's about your spirit dying. It's death in many forms:

- Spiritual death – where you lose intimacy with God
- Emotional death – where your peace, joy, and purpose fade
- Relational death – where dysfunction replaces divine connection
- Mental death – where confusion, depression, and torment settle in
- Physical consequences – including disease, breakdown, and destruction of your body
- Eternal death – eternal separation from God in hell

Yes, hell is real. And yes, people still go there. Not because God wants them to, but because they refused to repent.

I could sense that my spirit was dying when I realized I was drawn more to carnal pleasures than to spiritual fulfillment. This shift was evident in my reactions, responses, and even in how I carried myself. While I wasn't acting wild and reckless, I recognized that my spirit was weak because I lacked discipline over my desires. I continued to indulge in ungodly behaviors, living a lifestyle that was outside of God's will.

I was lukewarm. The Bible says that being lukewarm is the worst state of all, because, as previously mentioned, you must be one or the other, hot or cold. If you're somewhere in the middle, the Lord says He will spew the lukewarm out of His mouth (Revelation 3:16).

I didn't feel spiritual, even though I was still going to church, and serving. While still being a side piece, I was feeding my flesh more than my spirit. And the more I did, the more fear grew inside of me. The constant fear of dying and going to hell was one of the clearest signs to me that my spirit was dying.

A dying spirit means a lack of discipline, a lack of control, a life given over to lustful desires instead of God's will. I gave life to death, and the wages of sin, instead of feeding life into my spirit man. My spirit was suffocating, gasping for air, crying out for revival.

Revival started with acknowledgment. I had to admit that my spirit was dying. Once I confessed it and faced the truth, God made it clear what I had to do. And even though it wasn't easy, it was possible, because God's grace and mercy met me in my brokenness and began the work of restoration.

You Can't Live in Sin and Claim Christ

1 John 3:9 (NLT) "Those who have been born into God's family do not make a practice of sinning, because God's life is in them."

This scripture doesn't say we'll never mess up, but it makes it clear: practicing sin is not the life of a true believer. If you say you love Jesus but choose to stay in sexual sin, you're not in agreement with Him; you're at war with His Word.

You can't say you're His and still:

- Sleep with someone else's husband
- Share your body outside of the covenant

- Live in a "situationship" of sexual compromise
- Entertain sin with no conviction or correction

John 14:15 (KJV) "If ye love me, keep my commandments."

Love for Jesus will always lead to obedience.

There Is Still Grace-But Grace Requires Change

Some will say, "But God is merciful."

Yes, He is. But mercy is not permission. And grace is not an excuse to keep sinning.

Romans 6:1–2 (NIV) "Shall we go on sinning so that grace may increase? By no means! We are those who have died to sin; how can we live in it any longer?"

God's grace pulls us out; it does not pat us on the back and let us stay. Grace empowers change. Grace covers your past, but it also calls you to a higher place.

So, What Does Change Look Like? What Are The Steps?

For me, one of the very *first steps* were taking accountability. I had to realize and accept where I was at that particular time in my life. I couldn't sugarcoat it. I couldn't make excuses. I had to confess the truth. I admitted with my mouth that I was living in sin. I said it out loud: "I am a side piece. I am a mistress. I am not living the life God called me to live."

That confession was painful, but it was necessary.

That's why the first step to change is accountability. You can't repent for what you won't admit. You can't be free from what you won't call out for what it truly is.

The *second step* was repentance. Accountability acknowledges the sin; repentance turns away from it. Repentance is more than feeling sorry; it's asking God for forgiveness and making a conscious decision to leave the sin behind. I had to repent not only for the things I did, but also for the pain I caused; to myself, to others, and most of all, to God.

Repentance, like sin, is a process. I said earlier that becoming a side piece wasn't something I just accepted outright; it was a process of compromise that I allowed myself to fall into. In the same way, change is a process of surrender, one step at a time.

Step one: Admit your wrong.

Step two: Repent and ask God's forgiveness.

Step three: Rededicating your life back to God.

Yes, repentance is acknowledging your sin and asking for forgiveness, but rededication is an intentional surrender. It's standing before God and declaring again that Jesus Christ is your Lord and Savior.

That's what I had to do. After I admitted my wrong and repented, I rededicated my life back to Him. I said, "Lord, I can't do this without You. Come back into my life and use me according to Your will." It wasn't about empty words; it was about giving Him access again, permitting Him to rebuild me, to heal me, and to realign me with His purpose.

Rededication is powerful because it shifts your posture from shame to surrender. It's saying, "God, I may have failed, but I'm still Yours. Use me despite my past."

Step four: Renewal.

Renewal means feeding your spirit with God's Word, prayer, and daily worship. When I was going through the process of change, I had to renew both my mind and my heart. That meant going deeper into His Word, praying more, and worshiping daily.

That renewal started with small things. Waking up in the morning, the first thing I would do was thank God that I was alive and breathing and ask Him to use me according to His will. Renewal meant setting aside time every day to read and meditate on His Word. And I didn't just read anything, I sought out the scriptures that reminded me of who I am in Christ. I needed the Word to reshape my identity and remind me that I wasn't just a side piece, I was God's daughter.

Some of the scriptures that carried me through renewal were:

- *Romans 12:2 – "Be not conformed to this world: but be ye transformed by the renewing of your mind..."*
- *2 Corinthians 5:17 – "Therefore if any man be in Christ, he is a new creature: old things are passed away; behold, all things are become new."*
- *Ephesians 4:22–24 – "...put off concerning the former conversation the old man, which is corrupt according to the deceitful lusts; and be renewed in the spirit of your mind; and... put on the new man, which after God is created in righteousness and true holiness."*
- *1 Peter 2:9 – "But ye are a chosen generation, a royal priesthood, a holy nation, a peculiar people; that ye should shew forth the praises of him who hath called you out of darkness into his marvelous light."*

- *Psalm 139:14 – "I will praise thee; for I am fearfully and wonderfully made..."*

But renewal isn't only about reading and praying; it's about God literally changing your desires.

At first, I tried to walk away from sin in my own strength. I convinced myself that I was done. I told myself I was angry and didn't want to be a side piece anymore. But within a week, I would start missing him and fall back into the same cycle. That's because willpower can't deliver you. Flesh can't conquer flesh.

It wasn't until I fully surrendered that God's strength carried me. And it was amazing how He worked. His Spirit didn't just comfort me; it overtook my flesh. God literally slapped the taste out of my mouth for the very thing I had been doing for so long.

The Lord cut the desires out of me. He made the relationship that once consumed me feel sour, distasteful, and shameful. What once held me no longer had power over me. I was no longer bound by sexual immorality, loneliness, or rejection. Renewal wasn't just about discipline; it was about deliverance.

And that's what I want people to know: when you truly submit to Him, God can literally rewire your desires. He can make you hate the very thing that once kept you bound. Renewal is His Spirit reviving your spirit and breaking every chain.

But renewal didn't stop there.

Another part of being renewed in spirit and mind was seeking counseling and guidance. For too long, I had believed the saying, “What goes on in this house stays in this house.” That mindset made me hide, suffer silently, and stay stuck.

Counseling gave me space to sort out my insecurities. It helped me re-evaluate my thought process. It kept me from focusing only on the wrong things and allowed me to see things through a healthier lens. And it gave me accountability for both my ungodly actions and my godly growth.

I would absolutely recommend that part of renewal involves seeking wise, godly counseling and guidance. God places people in our lives to strengthen us, encourage us, and help us stay on track. Renewal doesn’t happen in secrecy; it happens in honesty, openness, and accountability.

Step five: Taking one day at a time.

When I was going through my change, I quickly learned that every day wouldn't feel the same. Some days I felt strong and hopeful, but other days I felt weak, down, or discouraged. On those harder days, I had to draw from what I had learned in counseling, put those lessons into perspective, and remember how to cope in healthy, godly ways.

I also had to lean on prayer daily, asking the Lord to guide me one day at a time. Sometimes it wasn’t just daily; it was hourly, even minute-by-minute. Taking it one day at a time reminded me that this was a process, not a sprint.

Pacing myself was key. Instead of trying to fix everything all at once, I surrendered each day to God. One prayer at a time. One decision at a time. One victory at a time. And I would recommend the same for anyone going through change: don't rush it. Take it one step, one day, one moment at a time.

But what if you've never even thought about changing?

Maybe you've been living this way so long that it feels normal. Maybe you've convinced yourself that it's "just who you are." Or maybe you've been afraid of what change would cost you. But here's the truth: if God did it for me, He can do it for you.

It starts with a whisper: "Lord, I need You."

It starts with one small act of honesty: "God, I can't do this without You." And from there, He will meet you right where you are.

You don't have to have it all figured out. You don't have to clean yourself up first. You have to be willing because the same God who gave me grace will give you grace, too.

Change begins the moment you invite Him in.

Hell Is Real- But So Is Heaven

Galatians 5:19–21 (NLT) "When you follow the desires of your sinful nature, the results are very clear: sexual immorality, impurity, lustful pleasures... Let me tell you again... that anyone living that sort of life will not inherit the Kingdom of God."

Let that settle in.

You can miss Heaven living in sexual sin.

This isn't just about "bad choices" or "low moments." This is about eternity. Your body might feel good in the moment, but your soul is crying out for deliverance.

God is not playing with sin. We shouldn't either.

BUT THERE'S STILL TIME TO TURN

The beautiful thing about the Gospel is that it always comes with a chance to repent.

Romans 6:23 "For the wages of sin are death; but the gift of God is eternal life through Jesus Christ our Lord."

You don't have to die in sin. You don't have to stay stuck in cycles. You don't have to keep pretending you're okay.

You can come out. You can come home. You can be restored, renewed, and redeemed.

God is not looking for perfection. He's looking for repentance.

Repentance began when I realized it was time to turn. But I want to be honest: my first attempt to walk away failed.

A week would pass, and I would start missing him. The loneliness would creep in. The feelings I had for him would resurface. And before I knew it, I was right back in the same trap, repeating the same cycle.

That's because anger can't deliver you. Willpower can't sustain you. Flesh can't overcome flesh.

It wasn't until I became completely exhausted - exhausted in my soul, exhausted in my spirit, and weary of trying to fix myself, that I cried out to the Lord and said, "God, if I'm going to change, You have to change me. I can't do this on my own. I am willing to fully submit to You."

That's when true repentance began for me. Not when I tried to walk away in my own strength, but when I surrendered and let God's strength carry me.

And it's amazing how God works. His strength doesn't just cover you; it overtakes your flesh. When I say that the Lord can literally slap the taste out of your mouth for something you've been doing for so long, I mean it. That's exactly what happened to me when I truly submitted.

God created a separation, and not just physical separation, but spiritual separation. Over time, He cut the desires out of me. What I once craved, I no longer wanted. What I once missed, I no longer longed for. He literally took the taste of being a side piece away from me.

The thought of the relationship that once consumed me began to sour my mouth. It made me cringe. And for a long time, it also made me feel shame, something I'll talk more about later in this book.

But here's the truth: God can do anything. He can deliver, He can heal, and He can change a person completely. He did it for me.

God changed me in a way that freed me from bondage. I was no longer chained to sexual immorality. I was no longer held by loneliness. I was no longer trapped by rejection. I didn't feel those things anymore. Instead, I felt conviction and sorrow for what I had done, and I couldn't understand how I had let myself get into that situation in the first place.

But even in that sorrow, I was free. Because shame didn't bind me, God used it to humble me. And through that humbling, He birthed my healing.

Reflection of Chapter Four:

Sin is not just a mistake; it's a master if you don't break free.

You cannot love Jesus and still love sin. Being a side piece, just a piece, or living in sexual sin isn't just hurting you; it's separating you from God. And if you stay in it, the end is death.

But if you turn, repent, and come back to Him, there is life, and life more abundantly.

A Blueprint for Change

Change doesn't happen overnight. It is a process, but it begins with one decision: the decision to live no longer bound to sin. Here are the five steps that helped me, and that can help anyone ready to walk into freedom:

1. Accountability – Admit where you are. Be honest with yourself and with God. Call sin what it is. Don't excuse it, don't sugarcoat it, confess it. I had to admit out loud: "I'm living in sin. I'm a side piece. This is not who God called me to be." That confession was painful, but it was necessary.
2. Repentance – Once you admit the truth, turn from it. Repentance isn't just saying "I'm sorry." It's asking God for forgiveness and making a conscious decision

to walk away. My first attempts failed because I relied on my own strength. I told myself I was angry and didn't want the relationship anymore, but within a week, I'd fall back. It wasn't until I surrendered and said, "Lord, I can't do this without You-You have to change me," that true repentance began.

3. Rededication – After repentance, surrender your life back to God. Acknowledge again that Jesus Christ is your Lord and Savior. Invite Him back in and give Him full access to rebuild, heal, and use you for His glory. I had to say, "Lord, I'm Yours again. Come into my life and use me according to Your will."
4. Renewal – Renewal means feeding your spirit with God's Word, prayer, and daily worship. I began each morning with thanksgiving, asking God to use me. I set aside time to read His Word and meditate on scriptures that reminded me of who I am in Christ. Verses like Romans 12:2, 2 Corinthians 5:17, and Psalm 139:14 helped reshape my identity.

But renewal isn't only about discipline; it is about deliverance. At first, I tried to leave on my own strength, but I kept going back. When I fully submitted, God's strength carried me. As I stated earlier, He literally slapped the taste out of my mouth for what once consumed me. The relationship that had once felt so sweet suddenly became sour. The very thought of it made me cringe. God cut the desire at the root.

That's what renewal does: it revives your spirit, breaks the chains, and rewires your desires. What once enslaved you no longer has power over you. Renewal is God's Spirit breathing life into your spirit and restoring wholeness.

Renewal also came through seeking counseling and guidance. For too long, I believed the lie, "What goes on in this house stays in this house." But counseling helped me sort through insecurities, reframe my thinking, and stay accountable. Renewal isn't done in secrecy; it's built through openness, support, and godly community.

5. Take One Day at a Time – Finally, change is a daily journey. Some days felt victorious, while others felt heavy. I had to pace myself. Some days it was one prayer at a time, one hour at a time. Taking it one day at a time reminded me that God doesn't demand perfection. He wants progress.

Chapter Four Prayer: A Prayer of Repentance and Restoration

Father God,

I've heard Your truth, and I feel the weight of Your Word—no more excuses. No more pretending. No more calling sin "a mistake." I come before You with honesty and humility, repenting for every sin I've committed in my body and in my heart.

Forgive me, Lord, for walking in disobedience. Forgive me for ignoring Your Word while claiming Your name. Forgive me for living in ways that grieve Your Spirit. I repent. I turn. I surrender.

Break every ungodly habit. Deliver me from sexual sin. Wash me clean from the inside out. I choose holiness. I choose righteousness. I choose obedience. Not just because I fear death, but because I desire life in You.

Thank You for giving me another chance. Thank You for the cross. Thank You for grace. I choose to walk out of sin and into Your marvelous light.

In Jesus' name,
Amen.

Chapter Five: I Was On My Way To Hell-But Grace Found Me Whole

I know what it's like to want to do right but still live wrong.

I know what it's like to be in church-faithfully, present, serving, and still feel the pull of flesh. I know what it's like to lift my hands in worship and lower my standards in private. I know what it's like to call on Jesus but still entertain relationships He never authorized.

I felt divided: righteous in public but compromised in private.

And while I wasn't trying to be a side piece, or even just a piece, I was still living outside of covenant. I was still giving myself to people who didn't have God's permission to access me. I was walking, talking, praising, and sinning, and I was on my way to hell.

Let me say that again for the woman who thinks she can still play with grace:

I was on my way to hell.

The season in my life, when I was a side piece, deep down in my spirit, I knew that I was living outside the will of

God. Yet, I was still trying to operate as though I was spiritually whole. Looking back, I realize just how much I took God's grace and His mercy for granted. I misused them. I abused them. I stretched them thin, thinking they would always be there to cover me while I continued doing what I wanted to do.

Even in my brokenness, I kept ushering. I kept praising. I kept moving in positions that required spiritual integrity, even though I was completely out of alignment. Honestly, I should have sat down, paused, and allowed God to deal with, repair, and cleanse me. But I didn't want to be changed at the time. My flesh did not want to surrender. The Bible says plainly:

"The spirit indeed is willing, but the flesh is weak." — Matthew 26:41

And during that season, my flesh was running the show.

One of the greatest indicators of how far gone I was spiritually was the way I handled Holy Communion. Taking communion is sacred. It is not something to play with. Scripture warns us clearly:

"Let a man examine himself, and so let him eat of that bread, and drink of that cup." — 1 Corinthians 11:28

Yet I convinced myself that if I just asked God to forgive me right before communion, I could still participate, even though I had no real intention of changing. So, every first Sunday, while living in sin, I took communion as if I were right with God.

I had reduced repentance to a quick apology.

There was no true turning away. No brokenness. No conviction. Just convenience. But the Word reminds us that true repentance requires true change:

"Repent therefore, and be converted, that your sins may be blotted out." — Acts 3:19

Part of me also felt that if I didn't take communion, people would notice. They would look at me. They would wonder. So, I used the Lord's Supper as a cover-up and convinced myself that a last-minute "Lord, forgive me" made me worthy.

But scripture warns that taking communion unworthily brings danger to the soul:

"For he that eateth and drinketh unworthily, eateth and drinketh damnation to himself." — 1 Corinthians 11:29

And that's exactly what I was doing, inviting spiritual consequences while pretending to be holy.

The Lukewarm Coffee Analogy

What I didn't realize, until later on, was that spiritually, I had become lukewarm. I wasn't hot; I wasn't cold. I was comfortable in sin but still wanted the appearance of righteousness.

It's just like when someone orders coffee.

Some people love their coffee piping hot. Others prefer iced coffee. But nobody-nobody-asks for lukewarm coffee. Lukewarm coffee is unpleasant. It's unsatisfying. When people receive lukewarm coffee instead of what they ordered, they pour it out, send it back, add ice to make it cold, or heat it to make it hot. Why?
Because lukewarm doesn't satisfy anybody.

And spiritually, lukewarm Christians don't satisfy God.

The Bible says:

"I know thy works, that thou art neither cold nor hot... So then because thou art lukewarm, and neither cold nor hot, I will spue thee out of My mouth." — Revelation 3:15–16

That was me. My life had become spiritually lukewarm. I was neither walking boldly in sin nor standing boldly in righteousness. I was floating between both worlds, pretending that God would accept what He clearly rejected.

My mindset was spiritually sick. I was playing a dangerous game, removing myself from under God's covering while thinking I was still protected. Scripture warns:

"If we sin willfully after we have received the knowledge of the truth, there remaineth no more sacrifice for sins." — Hebrews 10:26

That was me– willfully sinning, willfully disobedient, willfully choosing, flesh over God. I was on my way to hell, not because God desired that end for me, but because I was choosing the path that led there.

Yet even in all of that, His mercy still reached me.

God allowed me to come to a place of true repentance-not the kind I forced out of fear of being exposed, but the kind that rises from a broken, humbled, surrendered heart. Scripture says:

"The Lord is nigh unto them that are of a broken heart; and saveth such as be of a contrite spirit." — *Psalm 34:18*

He allowed me to see the true condition of my soul. He opened my eyes to the danger I was in. He showed me that playing with holy things while living unholy was not only dangerous, but it was also deadly. Standing in the aftermath of that night when my entire life flashed before my eyes, a moment where I could have lost my life, I could not escape one undeniable truth: God had spared my life.

That night forced me to confront the reality of where my choices had taken me. What I once justified as love had placed me in a position that almost cost me everything.

It was my wake-up call! It was the moment when I realized that the life I was living was not the life God intended for me.

And yet, after all of that, He still loved me enough to pull me out.

He still covered me. He still spared me.

"It is of the Lord's mercies that we are not consumed... great is Thy faithfulness." — *Lamentations 3:22–23*

I thank God for His patience. I thank Him for not letting me die in my mess. I thank Him for giving me another chance, not only to repent, but to truly change, truly grow, and truly walk in the freedom and righteousness He intended for me.

I thank Him for saving me... even when I was not trying to save myself.

What It Really Means to Be Lukewarm Saved

Many of us are lukewarm saved. We go to church, sing in the choir, even pay tithe and offering, and then we sin on purpose. If this is not lukewarm, then I do not know what is!

Many of us would hear the Word on Sunday and deliberately disobey God on Monday. I know this firsthand. That was me. I was living a hypocritical life. I was a lukewarm Christian because I chose to stay in my sin. But God loved me so much. He allowed my world to shake to get me back on track.

I am not only speaking from personal experience. Scripture confirms this truth through the lives of many of God's chosen vessels. Their stories show us that salvation does not eliminate weakness, nor does a calling eliminate the consequences of disobedience. How many of us know that when we choose to rebel against God, we are living in a state of lukewarmness? Let's look at one of God's chosen vessels, Jonah.

Jonah-Called, But Running From God

(Reference: Jonah 1-4)

Jonah was a prophet chosen by God, yet when God instructed him to go to Nineveh, he chose to rebel. He ran in the opposite direction, created storms for everyone around him, and ultimately ended up in the belly of a great fish (Jonah 1:17). To me, Jonah had fallen into a period of being lukewarm. Yet, it was God's grace and mercy, and His correction that pulled Jonah back into his rightful state.

Jonah was still called, even in his rebellious state.
God didn't abandon him; God allowed Jonah to be swallowed by a fish because Jonah's disobedience required correction.

That belly of the great fish was dark. It was confining. It was uncomfortable. Yet, it was correct.

Does this sound familiar?

You may never find yourself in the belly of a fish, but many of us have found ourselves in other "bellies."

Because in today's world, the belly of the fish doesn't always look miraculous. Sometimes it looks painful. Sometimes it looks embarrassing. Sometimes it looks destructive.

The belly of the fish may look like:

- A physical illness that came after ignoring God's warning.
- A sexually transmitted disease as a result of living outside of God's will.
- Emotional trauma from relationships God told you to leave.
- Domestic violence, manipulation, or control that started with disobedience.
- Broken families, lost trust, or spiritual numbness.
- Cycles of shame, regret, and consequences that didn't just affect you, but everyone connected to you.

Just like Jonah's disobedience didn't only impact him, but also the sailors on the ship. Our disobedience often creates a domino effect. What we choose doesn't stay contained. It spills over into our children, our spouses, our ministries, and our communities.

The belly of the fish is not always punishment; it is often correction.

God did not allow Jonah to remain there forever. The belly became a place of reflection, repentance, and realignment. Jonah prayed. Jonah acknowledged God. Jonah turned back.

And that is the key.

The belly is not meant to destroy you; it is meant to redirect you.

But here's the question every reader must answer for themselves:

- What does your belly of the fish look like?
- What consequence are you currently living with that may have come from disobedience?
- What warning did God give you that you ignored?
- Who else has been affected by your choices?
- Are you praying inside the belly, or resisting correction?
- What step of repentance or obedience is God asking you to take right now?

When I ask you what your belly of the fish looks like, I am not asking a question I have not had to answer myself.

For me, the belly of the fish was not sickness.
It was not shame. It was not confusion.

My *belly of the fish* was being a side piece.

And it almost destroyed me.

Physically, it drained me.
Mentally, it tormented me.
Emotionally, it broke me down piece by piece.

I lived in a place of constant inner conflict, knowing better, yet doing what I knew was outside of God's will. The weight of secrecy, the stress of hiding, the emotional tug-of-war between conviction and desire...it all took a toll on my body. I was exhausted in ways sleep could not fix. My peace was gone, and my spirit was heavy.

Mentally, I was not whole. I questioned my worth. I battled confusion. I wrestled with guilt and justification at the same time. I knew God, but I was not obeying God, and that contradiction created chaos within me.

And that chaos did not stay with me alone.

Just like Jonah's disobedience affected everyone on the ship, my choices affected entire families.

Being a side piece did not just wound me, it interrupted family life. It caused division, pain, mistrust, and heartbreak on both sides. Relationships were strained. Homes were disrupted. Innocent people were hurt. What I thought was "my situation" became everyone's suffering.

That was my belly of the fish.

It was dark.
It was isolating.
It was painful.
And it was suffocating.

The belly I was in was the consequence of ignoring God's warnings and continuing in a place He never assigned me to be. I did not fall into it accidentally. I stayed in it knowingly. And the longer I stayed, the more damage I caused.

The belly of the fish, for me, looked like:

- Emotional instability
- Spiritual distance from God
- Broken trust
- Collateral damage to families
- A loss of peace I could not explain away

And the most dangerous part of the belly is this:
You can survive long enough in it to normalize it.

But surviving is not living.

And surviving in disobedience is still dying, just slowly.

What finally shifted for me was understanding that God was not trying to destroy me. He was trying to correct me. The belly was not proof that God had abandoned me. It was proof that He loved me enough to stop me.

The belly became my place of awakening.
My place of repentance.
My place of surrender.

And just like Jonah, I had to cry out from the very place my disobedience put me.
If my belly of the fish was being a side piece, what is yours?

What place are you in right now that God never intended for you to live in?

What situation is costing you your peace, your health, your family, or your spiritual clarity?

What pain are others carrying because of a choice you continue to justify?

The belly will not last forever, but staying in disobedience can prolong it.

Deliverance begins when honesty starts.

Freedom begins when obedience returns.

And healing begins when you decide that the belly is no longer where you belong.

You don't get out of the belly by blaming others.
You don't get out by justifying sin.
You don't get out by pretending it doesn't hurt.
You get out by turning back to God.

Jonah came out of the fish changed, humbled, and recommissioned. And the same God who commanded the fish to swallow Jonah is the same God who commanded the fish to release him.

Your belly does not have to be your burial place.
It can become your turning point.

Moses-Favored, Anointed, But Acting in His Flesh

(Reference: Numbers 20:7–12)

Moses had intimate access to God and was used in miraculous ways. When God told him to speak to the rock, Moses struck it instead, allowing anger and frustration to override obedience. Water still flowed because God is faithful, but Moses lost something precious. He was allowed to see the Promised Land, but not enter it. Moses was saved and chosen, but his moment of disobedience cost him a promise.

David-After God's Heart, Yet Driven By Desire

(Reference: 2 Samuel 11–12)

David was a man after God's own heart (1 Samuel 13:14), yet even he fell into sin. His desire for Bathsheba led to adultery, deceit, and the death of an innocent man. God forgave David after his repentance (Psalm 51), but his household still endured devastating consequences (2 Samuel 12:10–14).

David loved God, but even love does not exempt us from the consequences of disobedience.

Samson-Anointed From Birth, But Destroyed By His Weakness

(Reference: Judges 13–16)

Samson's story is a powerful example of someone who was chosen, consecrated, and supernaturally gifted. Yet his weakness for ungodly relationships, specifically Delilah, opened the door to deception and destruction. Delilah repeatedly manipulated him, yet Samson trusted her because his flesh was louder than his discernment. When he revealed the secret of his strength, he lost far more than his hair:

- He lost his power.
- He lost his vision.
- He lost his freedom.
- He lost his divine position.

Samson didn't fall because he wasn't chosen. He fell because he hadn't surrendered.

The Lesson in All Their Stories

- Jonah ran from God. (Jonah 1–4)
- Moses acted in anger. (Numbers 20)
- David acted in lust. (2 Samuel 11)
- Samson acted in weakness. (Judges 16)

Each of them was:

- called
- loved
- chosen
- anointed
- used by God

Yet each still fell into sin.

Their lives teach us:

- Being saved does not prevent temptation.
- Being called does not guarantee obedience.
- Being anointed does not replace discipline.
- Being gifted does not eliminate consequences.
- Being chosen does not protect us from our choices.
- You can know God intimately and still rebel.
- You can be powerful publicly but weak privately.
- You can be spiritually gifted but emotionally undisciplined.
- You can be saved but still living in sin.

Why This Matters for My Story

Like Jonah, I ran from what I knew was right.
Like Moses, I let emotions override obedience.
Like David, I allowed desire to lead me.
Like Samson, I trusted something that was destroying me.
I was saved, but not surrendered.
Loved, but misaligned.
Chosen, but walking outside of God's will.
And just like God corrected them, He corrected me.
Not to harm me, but to save me from myself.

His discipline was mercy.

His conviction was grace.

His correction was love.

Being Saved Does Not Exempt Us from Judgment

There is something vital that every believer must understand:

Being saved does not exempt you from consequences.
Being saved does not give you a free pass to live however you want. Being saved does not excuse sin, justify sin, or protect you from the judgment of God if you refuse to repent and turn away from the things that separate you from Him.

Grace is powerful. Grace is beautiful. Grace is a gift.
But grace is not permission.

The Bible tells us plainly:

"Shall we continue in sin, that grace may abound? God forbid." — Romans 6:1–2

In other words: *Don't think grace gives you the right to keep sinning.*

You can be saved and still be judged. You can be saved and still be disciplined by God. You can be saved and still lose blessings, peace, opportunities, and protection. You can be saved and still drift far from God.

You can even be saved and still go to hell if you refuse to repent.

People don't like to talk about that part, but it is the truth of God's Word.

Salvation is a covenant, not a cover-up. Grace is an invitation to change, not permission to continue in sin. Jesus Himself warned that not everyone who calls Him "Lord" will enter the Kingdom of Heaven:

"Not every one that saith unto me, Lord, Lord, shall enter into the kingdom of heaven; but he that doeth the will of my Father which is in heaven." — Matthew 7:21

Calling Him Lord is not enough. Going to church is not enough. Serving in ministry is not enough. Saying you are saved is not enough.

If your lifestyle, your choices, and your behavior contradict the Word of God, then you are in spiritual danger, even if you are a believer.

The Bible teaches that habitual, unrepentant sin leads to spiritual death:

"For the wages of sin is death..." — Romans 6:23

And spiritual death leads to eternal separation from God.

We shout about blessing but overlook the truth:
Hell is real. And believers are not exempt. Not because God

doesn't love us, but because He is holy. Because He is just. Because He cannot reward rebellion.

Refusing to repent...Refusing to turn from sin...Refusing to surrender...puts us at risk even as believers.

Salvation is the doorway, but obedience is the path.
Grace opens the door, but repentance keeps us inside.
Mercy gives us time, but surrender gives us life.

So yes, we are saved. Yes, we are loved. Yes, God is merciful.

But His mercy is meant to lead us to repentance, not complacency.

"God's kindness is intended to lead you to repentance." —
Romans 2:4 (NIV)

Because the truth is: If we willingly choose sin, knowingly reject His voice, and stubbornly refuse to turn from the things He is calling us out of, we are choosing separation from God, and separation from God in this life leads to separation from God in eternity.

This is why obedience matters. This is why surrender matters. This is why repentance matters.

Being saved does not mean you cannot lose your way.
Being saved does not mean grace will always shield you from consequences. Being saved does not mean you are immune to judgment.

And being saved does not guarantee heaven if your heart refuses to follow God.

This is why I share my story so openly. I realized that, even as a believer, my choices could have cost me everything. Not just my peace, not just my purpose, not just my blessings, but my soul.

I was saved but spiraling. I was saved but spiritually dying. I was saved but living in a way that could have carried me straight to hell.

Thank God for mercy. Thank God for grace. Thank God for another chance. I refuse to misuse that grace ever again, because now I know the truth:

- Salvation is the gift.
- Obedience is the proof.
- Repentance is the requirement.
- Holiness is the standard.
- Heaven is the reward.
- Hell is the consequence.

And both are real.

Before reality sank in, I was careless. I was selfish. I didn't think about the consequences of what I was doing. I was out there smiling, shouting, but spiritually sick. I didn't want to hurt anyone, but I was living in a way that not only hurt others and myself, but I also hurt my relationship with God.

Hurting God: The Relationship We Rarely Think About

When I think about the moment when I said, "I didn't want to hurt anyone, but I was hurting my relationship with God," I now realize something even deeper: I wasn't just hurting my relationship with God. I was hurting God Himself.

We don't often think of it that way.

When it comes to earthly, carnal relationships, we are quick to examine how we treat people. We think about how we've hurt others. We think about how they've hurt us. We think about how we mistreat ourselves. We spend so much emotional energy worrying about human feelings, yet we seldom stop to ask, "*What am I doing to God? How does this make Him feel?*"

We treat the Creator like an afterthought while elevating the creation.

But the truth is this:

Our actions can grieve God.

Our choices can wound His heart.

Our sin can make Him turn His face away.

The Bible tells us:

"And grieve not the Holy Spirit of God." — Ephesians 4:30

Grieve, meaning hurt, saddened, disappointed, to break His heart.

We talk about hurting people, but we almost never talk about how we hurt God, the One who gave us life, breath, identity, purpose, and destiny. The One who sees the beginning and the end. The One who knows our steps before we take them. The One who holds the whole world in His hands. The One who has blessed us far beyond what we deserve.

Yet when we are in sin, when we are living outside of His will, when we are doing things that He calls unholy, we rarely stop long enough to ask:

"God, does this hurt You?"

"Am I breaking Your heart?"

"Am I treating You the way You deserve to be treated?"

We worry about disappointing people...but we don't consider disappointing God. We worry about losing relationships...but we don't consider losing intimacy with Him. We worry about rejection from man...but not separation from His presence.

And yet, God is the One who blesses us daily, not just with the big things, but with blessings we take for granted: life, health, strength, breath, protection, and provision. He gives us more than enough. He gives us what we never earned. He gives us what we're not worthy of. And then, the greatest gift of all, He gave us His only Son.

"For God so loved the world, that He gave His only begotten Son..." —John 3:16

Jesus became the sacrifice so we wouldn't have to carry the penalty of sin ourselves. He took the nails, the stripes, the cross, for us. For me.

Yet even with that sacrifice, even with that level of love, we don't think about how our sin feels to God. We don't think about how our disobedience affects Him. We don't think about how our choices push Him away or bring dishonor to His holiness.

Because sin is not just wrong, it is relational.

When we sin, we are not just breaking rules; we are breaking God's heart.

We are not just stepping outside His will; we are stepping on His grace.

We are not just hurting ourselves; we are hurting the One who loves us most.

And that realization didn't hit me until much later, until God allowed me to see my behavior through His eyes, not my own. The pain I thought I was avoiding, the people I thought I was protecting, the feelings I thought mattered most were nothing compared to how I was hurting God through my sin...all in the name of being a sidepiece.

The question that remains is: Why don't we think about God first? Why don't we consider His heart the way we consider everyone else's? Why don't we treat our relationship with Him as sacred, tender, and fragile?

Maybe it's because truly seeing how we hurt God requires accountability, and accountability forces us to change.

But thank God for His mercy. Thank God for His patience. Thank God for loving us enough to reveal the truth.

Even when I was hurting Him, He still pursued me.
Even when I was grieving His Spirit, He still covered me.
Even when I gave Him every reason to walk away, He stayed.

That is love. That is grace. That is God.

Sometimes, when we are gifted, we believe that we are an exception, and the rules of adultery and fornication do not apply to us. There's a deception that creeps in when you're gifted. You think that because God still uses you, you're okay. But God doesn't bless rebellion. He extends mercy. His mercy was the only reason I didn't lose everything.

When people ask me, "*How did you know God showed mercy toward you?*" I can answer that question without hesitation. One of the greatest examples of God's mercy in my life was the way He surrounded me, even before my lowest, messiest, most sinful seasons, with family who prayed for me, covered me, and stood in the gap for me when I couldn't stand for myself, and even when they did not know what I was going through.

Despite everything I allowed to happen, despite the pain I caused others, and even the pain I inflicted on myself, God still placed a hedge around me through the people He assigned to my life. We don't talk enough about the self-inflicted pain; the pain we walk into willingly, the pain we choose because we ignore warning signs, the pain we cause ourselves through disobedience. That was the kind of pain I was in. But even there, God's mercy still found me.

I know God spared me in that season because of the prayers of my mother, my grandmother, my great-grandmothers, my sisters, my brothers, and even my church family at that time. I was covered when I wasn't living right. I was protected when my choices should have destroyed me. I was kept when I was choosing sin over God.

Those prayers were not ordinary prayers, they were intercessory prayers.

Somebody stood in the spiritual gap for me. Somebody travailed for me. Somebody called my name out before God when I wasn't calling His name for myself.

The Bible says:

"The effectual fervent prayer of a righteous man availeth much." —James 5:16

And I am a living witness to what it does.

I believe with everything in me that God extended grace to me because He remembered the prayers of the righteous women in my lineage-the matriarchs who carried spiritual weight. My mother prayed for all her children to be saved. My grandmother and great-grandmothers prayed for God to keep their children, grandchildren, and generations safe, covered, protected, and walking in the will of God.

And God honored their prayers.

Every one of my mother's children is saved, including me, not because we lived perfect lives, but because we were born into a lineage of intercession. A lineage of spiritually rooted women who knew how to touch heaven. A lineage of believers who sowed prayers long before I even knew I would need them.

Their prayers didn't just cover me; they preserved me.

The Bible says:

"The seed of the righteous shall be delivered."

— Proverbs 11:21

I am that seed.

I am that deliverance.

I am that answered prayer.

And even when I was walking in sin, even when I was lukewarm, even when I was playing with holy things while living unholy, their prayers kept me from falling so far that I couldn't get back up. Their prayers held me together when I was falling apart. Their prayers pulled me back to God when I was drifting farther away.

Sometimes we forget that if it hadn't been for the prayers of the righteous- the mothers, the fathers, the grandmothers, the aunties, the spiritual leaders, the intercessors- many of us would not be here today. Many of us would have died in our sins. Many of us would have been lost forever.

But because someone prayed, mercy met us. Because someone prayed, grace covered us. Because someone prayed, God kept us.

That is how I know God showed mercy toward me- because even when I didn't want Him, He still wanted me. And He proved it through the people He assigned to pray for me.

WHY GOD CHOSE MY FAMILY

The Lord revealed something else to me during my journey, and I believe this part is not only for me but also for many of my readers. Sometimes in life, we look at our family, the people God connected us to by blood and by lineage, and we silently ask ourselves, "Why did God place me here?

Why did He choose this family, this background, this generation, this tree for me?"

We question it because family isn't always perfect. We experience pain, misunderstandings, disappointments, and sometimes generational struggles that feel too heavy to carry. But the truth is this: God never makes a mistake. Everything He does is intentional, divinely ordered, and connected to His perfect will for our lives.

What we often fail to realize is that God places us in certain families because He knows what we will need before we even get there. He knows which family will produce prayer warriors. He knows which lineage will carry preachers, intercessors, prophets, encouragers, and spiritual anchors. He knows which household will instill strength, which grandmother will teach prayer, which mother will speak life, and which sibling will push you toward destiny even when they don't realize what they're doing.

So sometimes, even though we don't understand everything about the family we were born into, God does. And He knows what He is doing.

In my own life, I can look back now and see clearly why God placed me in my family. The prayers that covered me; the prayers of my mother, my grandmother, my great-grandmother, my siblings, the women and men of God who carried spiritual authority, were prayers spoken long before I even understood how much I would need them. They didn't always know what they were praying for, but God did. Their intercession became my protection. Their faith became my shield. Their cries before God became my lifeline.

And because of that, I know I'm in the right family. I know God did not make a mistake. I know I was planted exactly where I needed to be planted so that my destiny could unfold the way He intended.

So to my readers, if you've ever wondered, "Why was I placed in this family?" or if you've ever felt like you didn't belong or that you should have come from a different household, I want you to read this clearly: You are exactly where God wants you to be. You are not misplaced. You are not a mistake. You are not an accident of genealogy or birth order.

You were assigned to your family on purpose for God's ordained purpose.

And if you continue seeking Him, He will begin to show you the answers to your "why." He will help you understand the role your family plays in your calling, development, growth, and even healing.

This may seem like a small side note in the midst of this chapter, but the Holy Spirit pressed this into my heart for a reason, maybe for one specific reader who needs it, or maybe for many. As you walk through the process of understanding how you became a side piece or how you allowed yourself to settle for pieces, part of that understanding will come from recognizing your foundation, where you come from, who shaped you, and who prayed you through.

And even if there was confusion in your home, conflict in your childhood, or brokenness in your lineage, remember this:

"And we know that all things work together for good to them that love God, to them who are the called according to His purpose." — *Romans 8:28*

God will use your family-the good, the bad, the strong, the broken, the prayerful, the silent, the present, and even the absent-to push you toward your destiny. Nothing is wasted. No experience is accidental. And no family connection is random.

You are where you are for a reason...because God has a purpose for your placement.

It is because of all of this, I believe.

Grace Met Me.

I repented.

And I don't mean I just cried.

I don't mean I just felt bad.

I don't mean I just apologized after every night of compromise.

I mean, I turned.

I let it go.

I walked away from what I knew I shouldn't be in.

I laid down every soul tie, every habit, every person I let have access to me.

I asked God for His mercy, and He gave it. I asked God to help me, and He did.

Psalm 51:17 (NLT) "The sacrifice you desire is a broken spirit. You will not reject a broken and repentant heart, O God."

He didn't reject me. He received me. He restored me.

HOW I WALKED AWAY: IT WAS A PROCESS, NOT A MOMENT

When the question was asked, "How did you just walk away from living in sin or from being a side piece?" The honest answer is simple: I didn't just walk away. It didn't happen overnight. It wasn't instant. It wasn't a clean break.

As I mentioned earlier in Chapter 4, there were intentional steps I had to take. Deliverance was a process. Healing was a process. Clarity was a process. Understanding my worth was a process. Realizing God wanted more for me was a process.

And anyone reading this who has ever tried to walk away from something that had your emotions, your mind, and your flesh tied up knows exactly what I mean.

Walking away required more than willpower.
It required revelation.

One of the biggest revelations God gave me was the importance of understanding who I am and where I come from. We walk around struggling with different behaviors, cycles, and emotional patterns, especially when it comes to relationships, brokenness, and settling for less, but we rarely sit down and ask:

"Why am I this way?"

"Where did this behavior come from?"

"Is this truly me, or is this something I've inherited?"

Part of getting delivered from being a side piece, or from living beneath your worth in any form requires examining your background. Your lineage. Your family history. Your foundation. Because sometimes, if you study your family history long enough, you will begin to see "you" before you were even born.

- You'll see the patterns.
- You'll see the behaviors.
- You'll see the cycles.
- You'll see the similarities.
- You'll see the generational tendencies you unknowingly walked into.

And that's why the Bible tells us:

"Study to shew thyself approved..." — 2 Timothy 2:15

We study the Word of God, yes, but we also study ourselves in light of the Word. We examine our family history, our upbringing, our spiritual environment, and the generational patterns that may have shaped us.

The Bible speaks clearly about generational curses, cycles that pass-through families unless someone stands up, recognizes them, denounces them, and breaks them through the power of God. In the natural world, even history books confirm that certain behaviors and family tendencies repeat themselves over and over again. So, to get something different, you must first understand what you're fighting.

When I looked at my own history, I began to realize that some of what I was struggling with had roots deeper than I thought. And once I saw those roots, I also realized something else: I am not obligated to accept anything that does not line up with the Word of God.

If a behavior contradicts God's purpose for my life, I can denounce it.

If a cycle does not reflect God's holiness, I can break it.

If a pattern keeps me bound, I can reject it.

If it does not honor the calling on my life, I can cut it off.

Because Jesus didn't only die to save us. He died to free us.

When He hung on the cross, He broke every chain, every bondage, every curse, every stronghold. He broke the power of sin so that we no longer have to live in captivity. Jesus died so that we might live again, fully, freely, and in alignment with God's will.

So, no, I did not "just walk away" from being a side piece. It was a process.

There were roadblocks.
There were emotions.
There were moments of confusion.
There were setbacks.
There were days when my flesh wanted what God was trying to deliver me from.

But step by step, truth by truth, prayer by prayer, God gave me strength to walk away, not just physically, but spiritually, emotionally, mentally, and soul deep.

He didn't just remove me from the situation.
He removed the situation from my spirit.
He disconnected my appetite from it.

He broke the soul ties.
He healed the wounds that kept me going back.
He restored my identity.
He re-established my worth.

And by His grace and mercy, I didn't just leave the lifestyle; the lifestyle left me.

That is how I walked away.
Not by might, not by my own strength, but by the power of God working through a process that saved my life.

Knowing Who You Are-and Why It Matters After Deliverance

There is another truth I cannot leave out: it is essential to know who you are as an individual. Deliverance is not only about God pulling you out of something, it is also about God revealing who you were always meant to be. Once God delivers you, once He opens your eyes to the patterns in your history, once He exposes the generational cycles you were unknowingly repeating, the responsibility then shifts to you.

Because after deliverance, the enemy always tries to offer invitations back to bondage.

If we are not rooted in identity, if we don't know who we are, what we carry, and what God has freed us from, we run the risk of walking right back into the very thing God pulled us out of.

The Bible warns us of this:

"As a dog returneth to his vomit, so a fool returneth to his folly." — Proverbs 26:11

In other words:
If we knowingly go back to what made us sick, we will become sick again.

This is where understanding your lineage becomes vital. When you know which spirits, habits, tendencies, or generational struggles operate in your bloodline, you can recognize when something that is not God-sent is trying to get your attention. You can discern when something familiar is trying to lure you back into bondage.

Because once God provides a way of escape, willfully returning puts you in danger of re-entering the curse.

And the moment you step back into something God freed you from, you weaken your hedge of protection. You open spiritual doors. You reactivate generational patterns that God was trying to break. You invite warfare that could have been avoided.

That is why remaining free is just as important as getting free.

It requires wisdom.
It requires identity.
It requires discernment.
It requires boundaries.
It requires saying "no" to the familiar and "yes" to God.

Because the enemy will always use what feels familiar to pull you back. But identity-knowing who you are and whose you are-keeps you grounded in your deliverance. It reminds you that going back is not an option. It reminds you that freedom came at a price, Jesus' blood, and that your legacy, your purpose, and your destiny depend on staying out of the places God rescued you from.

What Repentance Will Do for You

I'm not writing this chapter as someone who has it all together. I'm writing as someone who knows what it's like to live in sin and then taste what it feels like to be free.

God didn't just clean me up. He changed my life.

- He made me whole again.
- He took my brokenness and made it into ministry.
- He gave me peace that wasn't tied to a man's approval.
- He healed my soul where I didn't even know I was bleeding.
- He blessed me with a husband, not just a man, but a covenant man.
- He realigned my life, spiritually, emotionally, and mentally.

What I once gave away to men who weren't mine, He gave back to me in purpose and protection.

The Blessing of Covenant Love

Let me be clear, marriage is not the prize. Obedience is.

But when you walk in obedience, God rewards you with what He knows you're ready for.

He gave me a husband, but more than that, He gave me honor. He gave me covering. He gave me a relationship that reflects the beauty of covenant, not confusion.

I know the difference now.

Being with someone "just because" and being with someone because God orchestrated it, there's no comparison.

I know what I have now in my marriage is a true covenant from God because from the very beginning, God was the center of our connection.

When my husband and I first came together, we were both still healing from our pasts. We still carried some insecurities and wounds, but the difference was that we both longed for God. We both wanted a marriage built on His foundation and His principles.

What makes my marriage different from any romantic relationship I had before is simple: we incorporate God into everything.

Every morning before leaving the house, we pray together. If we feel led during the day, we pause and pray again. We don't just bring God into the parts of our lives where it feels comfortable or convenient. We invite Him into every area. From our intimacy to our disagreements, from daily decisions to major life choices, God is present in it all.

My husband brings out the potential in me. He encourages me and pushes me toward God's will. And I do the same for him. Especially as a bishop, his calling is demanding, and as his wife, I share in those demands because we are one. That unity makes us strong, but what makes us unshakable is that God is the anchor of our marriage.

I can tell this marriage is different because of how I have changed. In past relationships, I wasn't always submissive, but with my husband, I honor him and respect him as the head of our home. I don't worship him; we worship God together. We both agree that God is the head; then comes man; then wife; then children; and then everything else follows. That order keeps us aligned.

Even in intimacy, I bring God into it. I pray that we continue to enjoy each other and honor the covenant He gave us. Because God made marriage sacred, and as the Word says, “the marriage bed is undefiled” (Hebrews 13:4).

What used to be sin outside of marriage has now become worship inside of covenant.

That is the difference. This marriage is not built on my flesh, my loneliness, or my desires. It is built on Christ, and because of that, it is whole.

- Covenant is sacred.
- Covenant is safe.
- Covenant is a mirror of Christ’s love.
- Covenant is worth waiting for.

I Can't Tell You What to Do-But I Can Tell You What It Cost Me

I’m not here to shame anyone. I’ve been there. I’ve been the one trying to stop, trying to get it right, trying to feel whole. I know how hard it can be.

I can’t tell you how to do it perfectly. I can’t tell you I never struggled.

But I can tell you this:

- When you give your body away without covenant, you give away your peace.
- When you let someone touch what God said is holy, you risk your destiny.

- When you choose momentary pleasure over obedience, you open the door to death.
- When you stay tied to someone who isn't yours, you walk further from who God says you are.

And when I tell you that no matter how far you've gone, God will welcome you home. I know this because the Bible says so.

Think about the story of the Prodigal Son (Luke 15:11–32). The younger son left his father's house, spent all his inheritance on wild living, and found himself broken, starving, and empty. But when he came to his senses, he realized he had to return home.

What happened when he returned? Despite his failures, despite his shame, and even though his older brother was angry and jealous, the father welcomed him with open arms. He clothed him, fed him, and celebrated his return.

That is how God is with us. Like the father in that story, He welcomes His children back with open arms. And just like the older brother, there will always be people-haters, naysayers, critics -who don't want to see you restored. They'll say, "Who are you that God would use you? Don't you remember what you did? Don't you know your past disqualifies you?"

But the truth is this: God's grace qualifies you. His forgiveness redeems you. His love restores you.

The Word says in John 3:16, *"For God so loved the world that He gave His only begotten Son, that whosoever believeth in Him should not perish, but have everlasting life."*

It is never too late until you breathe your last breath. While there is life in your body, there is still redemption. You can be forgiven. You can be restored. You can live again.

I know this to be true because God did it for me. He was there with open arms. He forgave me, restored me, and gave me new life. And He will do the same for you.

Now, you might ask me, "*How do you know?*"

I know because He did it for me. He restored me and gave me new life. When I was down and out, when I felt too far gone, He reminded me of the story of the prodigal son. And that reminder was enough for me to know that God is with me.

And if God is with me, who can be against me? (Romans 8:31).

You Are Not Just a Piece-You Were Made to Be Whole

To every woman reading this who feels stuck in compromise, you don't have to live there anymore.

I did. I survived it. But I also escaped it.

Not by my strength.

By His mercy.

If you feel like that's all you are, just a piece, just someone's backup plan, just someone he sees when he's bored, you've been lied to.

You are more than that. And if you repent, turn, and trust God, He will make you whole, too.

But maybe you're asking, "*How? How can I really become whole again?*"

If you're not sure where to start, I encourage you to go back and reread Chapter 4. In that chapter, I laid out the steps that God took me through, the Blueprint for Change: accountability, repentance, rededication, renewal, and taking it one day at a time. Those steps are not just words on a page. They worked for me, and I believe with all my heart they can work for you, too.

But here's the key: you have to be willing. Not just willing to try, but willing to do it. Be sincere. Go to God just as you are. Be transparent with Him, because He already knows what you're going through anyway. But when you admit it, when you take accountability, that's when God can step in. That's when He can begin to reshape, restore, and rebuild you into the person He always intended you to be.

Reflection of Chapter Five:

I am living proof that God restores what sin tried to destroy. I was on my way to hell because I loved sin more than God and because I didn't obey Him. John 14:15 states, "If you love me, you will keep my commandments". At one point, I convinced myself I loved God more, even while living the way I wanted to live. But grace met me in my mess. And now I walk in mercy, in wholeness, and in purpose.

You can, too.

Chapter Five Prayer: A Prayer of Thanks for Redemption and Wholeness

Father God,

Thank You for not leaving me where I was. Thank You for seeing my heart, even when my actions didn't match. Thank You for not letting me die in my sin. Lord, I repent for every way I lived outside of Your will. For every relationship, every soul tie, every compromise, every careless decision. I ask You to wash me, forgive me, and cleanse me.

I thank You for grace. I thank You for not letting my past be the end of my story. I thank You for another chance to live right, love well, and walk in purpose. Thank You for wholeness. Thank You for restoring my dignity, my purity, my voice, and my worth. And thank You for showing me that covenant is possible, and love Your way is better.

Help me use my story to free someone else.

In Jesus' name,
Amen.

Chapter Six: From Fragments to Favor

There are still days when I have to look at myself in the mirror and remind myself:
You are not who you used to be.

I do this because there are times when my past creeps back in. Sometimes I'll run into people who knew me back then, and they'll bring up old stories-things I did when I was living outside of God's will. Their words can sting for a moment. It's almost like the enemy tries to use those memories to drag me backward.

But then I have to stop and remind myself: That was the old me. That woman doesn't live here anymore.

I remember a time when someone who knew me during my side piece days laughed and joked about it as if it was still who I was. For a second, I felt the shame rise up in me, like I wanted to hide. But instead, I reminded myself of God's truth. I looked at myself in the mirror later that night and said, "You are redeemed. You are restored. You are not who you used to be."

And just like that, peace came over me. Because the truth is, my past no longer defines me. God defines me. His Word defines me. And when those old reminders come, I use them as a chance to give God glory, because every time I declare who I am now, I take back the power that shame used to have over me.

Here are some of the scriptures I stand on when I need to remind myself of my new identity in Christ:

- ***2 Corinthians 5:17*** – *"Therefore if any man be in Christ, he is a new creature: old things are passed away; behold, all things are become new."*
- ***Romans 8:1*** – *"There is therefore now no condemnation to them which are in Christ Jesus, who walk not after the flesh, but after the Spirit."*
- ***Isaiah 43:18–19*** – *"Remember ye not the former things, neither consider the things of old. Behold, I will do a new thing..."*
- ***Ephesians 2:10*** – *"For we are his workmanship, created in Christ Jesus unto good works, which God hath before ordained that we should walk in them."*
- ***Galatians 2:20*** – *"I am crucified with Christ: nevertheless I live; yet not I, but Christ liveth in me..."*

When I speak these scriptures aloud, they remind me who I am now: a child of God, made new, forgiven, and walking in purpose.

Yes, I've been through a lot. And truth be told, I've put myself through a lot, too. Some wounds weren't just inflicted on me; some were self-inflicted by the way I lived, the people I chose, and the things I accepted.

When you live a life outside of God's order, you don't just experience trauma, you start to devalue yourself. And with every compromise, every lie, every piece of yourself given away outside of covenant, you become fragmented.

A Life Lived Fragmented

For me, those compromises led to trauma. I dealt with the trauma of not walking in confidence. I carried the weight of never feeling whole. Each day felt the same, an empty routine, missing something. As a side piece or just a piece, I constantly felt like part of me was gone.

One of the deepest traumas I faced was the trauma of being labeled. To some, I was “his girl” or “his girlfriend.” Those names might sound flattering on the surface, but they were nothing more than illusions. They were mental hallucinations, words that covered up the truth. I was never his covenant partner. I was never his wife. I was a mistress, though the word was never spoken out loud.

Once I came to terms with the fact that I was a side piece, the label itself became a wound. It left me feeling less valued, as though I had to constantly compete to prove my worth. I asked myself over and over: “What can I do to make him choose me? What can I do to be enough? What can I do to be the only one?” That is trauma.

It was emotional trauma -the constant cycle of rejection and longing. It was spiritual trauma- because I knew I was living outside of God’s will but convinced myself it was acceptable. And it was identity trauma -because even when people around me complimented me, telling me how beautiful, kind, or talented I was, deep inside I didn’t believe it.

I had devalued myself. I didn't give myself a fair chance to stop and ask, "What do I have to offer as God's daughter? What is my worth in Him?" Instead, I settled for less, convincing myself I had to share what was never meant to be shared.

The irony of it all is that I was fully committed to him. I wouldn't share myself with anyone else. I gave all of myself to a man who only gave me half of himself. That contradiction alone was trauma.

Here's the truth: the trauma didn't disappear the moment I walked away. Trauma lingers. It lingers in your thoughts, in your emotions, in the way you see yourself. Even after leaving, I still carried the weight of rejection, insecurity, and shame. I still felt the ache of having given away pieces of myself that I could never get back.

That's the thing about trauma-you can leave the situation, but the situation doesn't always leave you.

And that's why healing can't come from willpower alone. It can't come from distraction, or time, or even new relationships. Healing comes from God. Only His love has the power to go deep enough to touch those broken places. Only His Spirit can breathe life into the places where your spirit feels dead.

Psalm 147:3 says, "*He healeth the broken in heart, and bindeth up their wounds.*" That's what He did for me. I was fragmented, traumatized, and empty, but God began to piece me back together again. Not just the surface parts that people could see, but the deep places no one else knew about.

Healing from trauma is a process, but it's possible when you place your wounds in the hands of the One who makes all things new.

But thank God, I didn't stay in fragments.
God met me in the pieces—and showed me favor.

The Show of Favor

When I say favor, I mean that He displayed His grace and mercy over my life in ways I could not have imagined. He allowed me to heal in a quiet place. He positioned me in a season when I could constantly hear His Word — not only in church but also through the Trinity Broadcasting Network (TBN). He made sure I was spiritually fed while He was mending me.

He restored me in my worship. When I returned to praise dance, He gave me the choreography, the movements, the liturgical expressions that flowed directly from His Spirit. He allowed me to usher again with joy. He showed me favor by surrounding me with people who embraced my imperfections and still loved me through my healing.

He allowed me to love again. And not just love — He allowed me to be loved. He gave me the favor of becoming the wife He called me to be. Through my husband, God showed me that I was still worthy to be cherished, honored, and loved as He intended in marriage.

His favor didn't stop there. He positioned me to love His people. He gave me empathy and compassion, not just for my own healing but so that I could go out and share the good news of Jesus Christ. He placed people in my path who came to me for spiritual guidance, and when I spoke, I spoke without condemnation. The shame that once silenced me was gone.

That's the kind of favor I'm talking about — the kind of favor that says, "Despite what you've been through, I will still use you. Despite your past, your story will still glorify Me."

That is the ultimate favor: to be chosen by God as a vessel, even after the brokenness, to still be able to witness His goodness and lead others to Him.

Identity Reclaimed: I'm Not Her Anymore

Every now and then, I run into people from my past—people who remember the "old me."

Some say things that try to resurrect who I used to be. When this used to happen in the early stages — before I was healed and while I was still walking through trauma — it would really bother me. In fact, it hurt deeply. On the outside, I would laugh it off or chuckle, but on the inside, I carried guilt and shame. I didn't know how to deal with those reminders because the wounds were still fresh.

But now, after God has walked me through the healing process, I can face those moments differently. When someone brings up the old me, I can smile and simply say, "Oh well."

But let me explain what that "oh well" means. It's not an "oh well" of bitterness, or dismissiveness, or pretending it doesn't matter. It's an "oh well" of confidence. An "oh well" that says, "That doesn't define me anymore. That person is gone. I don't live there anymore."

The "oh well" is a declaration of transformation:

- The old Lakisha is ***dead***.
- The new and improved Lakisha is ***here***.
- The healed, restored, favored Lakisha is alive and walking in ***God's purpose***.

It took time to get to this place. It wasn't overnight. Healing isn't instant — it's a process. But as I grew deeper in God's Word and closer to Him in prayer, I gained the confidence to face my past without fear.

They laugh at the memories, joke about the mess I made, and try to remind me of my worst seasons. I remember one incident very clearly. Someone brought up an explicit joke that I used to share with the man I was involved with. Back then, when the joke was first made, I laughed along. It was a dirty joke — sexual and inappropriate — but at the time, I entertained it because that was the nature of the relationship I was in.

But years later, when I was reminded of that same joke, I didn't laugh. I didn't smile. I just shook my head slightly and let it pass. The joke that once felt normal and funny to me now felt uncomfortable and out of place. I didn't care for it, and I didn't want to be associated with it.

That's how I knew God had truly changed me. He had removed the desire to laugh at what was dirty. What once seemed harmless "fun" now grieved my spirit. My reaction was no longer shaped by my flesh but by the Spirit of God working in me.

But you know what I do?

I shrug it off. I smile. And I remind myself: "That was the old me. This is the new me now."

2 Corinthians 5:17 (KJV) "Therefore if any man be in Christ, he is a new creature: old things are passed away; behold, all things are become new."

Now I can even laugh with people and say, "I must have bumped my head back then!" Not in shame, but in amazement at how far God has brought me. What others may see as a joke, I see as a testimony. Because every time I can say it with a smile, I'm declaring: "Look what the Lord has done. I am not who I used to be."

God made me new.

He forgave me. He cleansed me. He rebuilt me.

And He taught me how to walk in wholeness. I'm not the side piece. I'm not just a piece. I'm His daughter.

But part of me getting to this point — of truly knowing who I am to Him — was learning how to forgive myself.

God showed and taught me through His Word that He had already forgiven me. Over and over again, Scripture reminded me of His mercy:

- ***John 3:16*** – *"For God so loved the world, that he gave his only begotten Son, that whosoever believeth in him should not perish, but have everlasting life."*

- ***2 Chronicles 7:14*** – *"If my people, which are called by my name, shall humble themselves, and pray, and seek my face, and turn from their wicked ways; then will I hear from heaven, and will forgive their sin, and will heal their land."*

I knew God forgave me, but the harder part was forgiving myself. I kept replaying the shame, the guilt, the choices I made. I carried those mistakes like chains.

So, one day, I sat down with a piece of paper and wrote out everything that still held me in bondage — every failure, every label, every mistake. Then I tore that paper into pieces and threw it in the garbage. For me, that was an act of releasing, a symbol that I was no longer going to hold myself hostage for sins God had already forgiven.

That doesn't mean everyone has to do that exact act. But for me, it was a turning point. It was me saying, "I forgive you, Lakisha."

God reminded me that He alone is Judge. He alone forgives. He casts our sins into the sea of forgetfulness (Micah 7:19). So, if He can forgive me, who am I not to forgive myself? I am not bigger than God. And if the blood of Jesus covers me, then I have no right to hold myself to a punishment that God has already lifted.

This truth hit me hard. But once I embraced it, everything changed. Forgiving myself became a key part of my healing. It allowed me to move forward, to accept my past as just that — my past. I no longer wallowed in shame. I could talk about my story without fear.

That's why I can write this book today. Because God didn't just forgive me — He taught me to forgive myself. And that forgiveness opened the door for true freedom.

Walking in Purpose and Purity

I never imagined I'd be where I am now—a wife, a mother, a woman of God walking in peace, purpose, and purity.

He's taught me to serve Him first, to be a good wife, to love my family, and to use my story to help set other women free.

He taught me to serve Him first and to be a good wife, based on the promises in His Word.

Psalm 37 reminds me that "*If I delight myself in the Lord, He will give me the desires of my heart.*" And I've seen this come to pass in my own life. When I made the decision to truly serve Him first — not my flesh, not people, not even my own emotions — everything else began to fall into place. My marriage, my home, my family, my ministry — all of it started to align when I put God first.

As a wife, He has shown me, through Proverbs 31, what it means to be a virtuous woman. The Word tells us that her worth is far more precious than rubies. She is clothed in strength and dignity. She builds her home with wisdom. She works with willing hands. She provides peace, structure, and love for her household. She honors her husband, not by worshiping him, but by respecting him and supporting him as he walks in his calling.

This is how the Lord has taught me to love my family — not just through words, but through actions. His Word reminds me that love is patient, love is kind, love is sacrificial, love bears all things, believes all things, hopes all things, endures all things (1 Corinthians 13).

I've learned that living as a godly wife and mother doesn't mean perfection — it means partnership with God. When something bothers me in my home, in my marriage, in my business, or even within myself, the very first thing I do is take it to Him in prayer. That's the foundation of everything I am today: a relationship where He is always first.

Serving Him first has taught me how to speak with wisdom, how to hold my tongue when silence is better, how to love when it's hard, and how to forgive even when my flesh doesn't want to. Every lesson has come from His Word and His Spirit, guiding me step by step into who I am today.

There's a stillness in my soul now.

NOW, a STILL SOUL

That stillness looks like having a firm foundation — one that can't be shaken. It's stability in my mind, in my spirit, and in my soul. The stillness I now live in feels like freedom — freedom from the confusion, chaos, and emotional instability that once controlled me. It looks like peace, joy, and clarity. It looks like knowing my worth, walking in purpose, and resting in God's love.

My stillness is built on a solid foundation — not rocky, not fragile, but steady and sure. It's the peace of knowing that I am free, and that freedom has weight. It means I no longer have to fight for validation or chase love that was never meant for me. The stillness in my soul helps me guard the deliverance that God gave me, because now I can look back at where He brought me from without wanting to return.

When I reflect on how far I've come, that stillness reminds me that I can't go back. To go back would mean forfeiting the testimony that God has given me — the very story that proves His power. It would mean stepping back into bondage after being set free.

This stillness is also a mindset — a determination to do what's right instead of what's wrong. It's choosing holiness when temptation calls. It's choosing prayer over panic, worship over worry, purpose over pleasure. This stillness is the shift — the shift from my will to God's will. It's knowing that His plan for my life is better than anything I could have planned for myself.

Scripture Reflection:
"Be still, and know that I am God." — Psalm 46:10 (KJV)

When I allow myself to rest in Him, He reminds me that peace isn't the absence of problems; it's the presence of God.

And this stillness births peace. A peace I never had when I was living wild and unrighteously. A peace that the world can't understand or take away. This peace is not just calmness; it's the quietness of my soul even while chaos surrounds me. It's the assurance that no matter what's going on in the world, in the community, in the church, or even in my personal life — God is still in control.

This peace is connected to the stillness. It's that whisper from Heaven that says, "Be still." It's the quiet within the storm. The calm in the middle of confusion. And when I call out to God and say, "Lord, I need peace," He answers by silencing the noise inside of me before He silences the noise around me.

That peace reminds me that I belong to Him. It reminds me that even when the world feels loud, my spirit can rest. Because those who love the Lord can rest in knowing that everything will be okay — even when it doesn't look like it will.

Scripture Reflection:
"Be still, and know that I am God." — Psalm 46:10 (KJV)
Even in the storm, there is a peace that only His presence can bring.

Romans 12:1 (KJV)
"Therefore, I urge you, brothers and sisters, in view of God's mercy, to offer your bodies as a living sacrifice, holy and pleasing to God—this is your true and proper worship."

Purity is not just about not having sex—it's about knowing who you belong to. When I realized I belonged to God, I started to live like it.

I Belong To Him

It's not that I didn't know I belonged to God — I've always known it somewhere deep inside. But this time, it was different. It wasn't just head knowledge; it was revelation. It hit me — I don't belong to anyone but God. He is first, and He must be first in every area of my life.

It's amazing how you can grow up hearing about belonging to God, saying it in songs and in church, but never really grasp what that means until you've been through something. I subconsciously knew I was His, but I didn't live with the awareness of what that meant — not until I went through the change. Once I began walking through the process — the acknowledgement, the repentance, the rededication, the renewal, all those steps I mentioned earlier — it started to sink in.

I remember watching TBN faithfully — shows like Better Together and hearing messages from women like Joyce Meyer, Priscilla Shirer, and others who spoke truth and light into my life. As I listened, something in me began to shift. I didn't just hear the Word; I felt it working inside me. The more I heard, the more I realized that I wasn't just someone God loved. I was His daughter.

When that reality took hold, everything changed. I realized that belonging to God meant I didn't have to chase belonging anywhere else. It wasn't about being somebody's "piece" or "side." It wasn't even about being seen or chosen by man. I was already chosen — chosen by the King of Kings.

When I understood that, I also realized that everything God has belongs to His children. I'm an heir — not to the material things of this world, but to the spiritual treasures that can't be taken away. He gives me love, peace, joy, grace, mercy, and purpose. He gives me identity. He gives me Himself.

And that's the greatest inheritance I could ever have.

Scripture Reflection:

"The Spirit Himself beareth witness with our spirit, that we are the children of God: And if children, then heirs; heirs of God, and joint-heirs with Christ..."
— Romans 8:16–17 (KJV)

When you truly know who you belong to, you stop chasing temporary validation and start walking in eternal inheritance.

HOW TO SET BOUNDARIES AND DATE WITH DISCERNMENT

To every woman waiting on love: don't just wait—prepare.

Preparation isn't just about waiting for the right person — it's about becoming the right person. Becoming the woman that God is shaping you to be.

When I began preparing for my future spouse, I set short— and long-term goals. I wrote down things I wanted to accomplish for myself and things I prayed would be present in my future marriage. It wasn't about creating a perfect plan, but about positioning myself for purpose.

One of the best ways to prepare for love is to start by loving yourself. And before you can love yourself properly, you must fall in love with Christ. When you love Him first, you'll begin to see yourself the way He sees you — whole, valued, and worthy of godly love.

Take time to get to know yourself. Identify your weaknesses, acknowledge your strengths, and be honest about what still needs healing. Work on being a better version of you. Love yourself enough to grow. Learn to enjoy your own company. Treat yourself with kindness. Speak to yourself with grace.

Another important step is to surround yourself with healthy examples of godly marriage. Be around couples who love Christ and love each other. Watch how they handle challenges, communicate, and pray together. It's not about copying their every move — every marriage is different — but about learning what a God-centered relationship looks like.

If you desire marriage, align yourself with people who share that same vision. It's hard to prepare for covenant while consistently engaging in circles that only celebrate singleness without purpose. That doesn't mean isolating yourself — it just means being mindful of who feeds your perspective on love and life.

Preparing for marriage also means coming into it spiritually full, not spiritually empty. Bring your faith, your prayer life, your purpose, your gifts, and your anointing into the union. Be rooted in the Word of God. A great place to start is by studying Proverbs 31, the virtuous woman. Her life shows that godly preparation begins long before the wedding day — it begins with her relationship with God.

Preparation is an act of faith. It says, "Lord, I trust You enough to get ready even before I see what You're sending."

Preparation Scriptures for Women

Proverbs 31:10–12 (KJV)

"Who can find a virtuous woman? for her price is far above rubies. The heart of her husband doth safely trust in her, so that he shall have no need of spoil. She will do him good and not evil all the days of her life."

Ruth 3:11 (KJV)

"And now, my daughter, fear not; I will do to thee all that thou requirest: for all the city of my people doth know that thou art a virtuous woman."

Psalm 37:4 (KJV)

"Delight thyself also in the Lord: and he shall give thee the desires of thine heart."

1 Corinthians 7:34 (KJV)

"The unmarried woman careth for the things of the Lord, that she may be holy both in body and in spirit: but she that is married careth for the things of the world, how she may please her husband."

God doesn't want you to be passive; He wants you to be positioned.

And part of being positioned is setting boundaries.

Setting boundaries means letting your yes be yes and your no be no. It means being straightforward and consistent with your words. When you say something, mean it. Don't waver. Don't bend or sway to please others or to keep the peace when it costs you your spiritual safety.

I had to learn that boundaries require action — not just talk. It wasn't enough for me to say I had standards; I had to live them. Boundaries aren't suggestions — they're safeguards. They protect what God is building in you.

For me, that meant not allowing anyone to manipulate my mind or emotions, or entice me to break the very boundaries I set to protect my peace. When you set a boundary, you set it for a reason — usually because God revealed that something or someone was damaging your spirit. And once you set it, you must take it seriously.

In the Bible, we are reminded to "let your yea be yea and your nay be nay." (Matthew 5:37 KJV). That means standing firm in your decisions, especially those that protect your relationship with God.

When I decided to say no, I had to mean it — even when my emotions wanted to say yes. When I said yes to walking in purity and healing, I couldn't go back on that decision just because it got hard or lonely. I had to remind myself that my boundaries were not punishment; they were protection.

Setting boundaries is also an act of spiritual warfare. It tells the enemy, "You can't have access to me in this area anymore." It tells your flesh, "You no longer control my choices." And it tells God, "I'm serious about my healing."

When I learned to stand firm in my yes and my no, I found strength I didn't know I had. It built my confidence, my discernment, and my peace. Boundaries don't restrict you — they keep you free.

Scripture Reflection:

"But let your communication be, Yea, yea; Nay, nay: for whatsoever is more than these cometh of evil." — Matthew 5:37 (KJV)

Every boundary you honor becomes another layer of protection around the peace God has given you.

Here's what I've learned:

- Let him know up front: I'm saving myself for marriage.
- Don't apologize for your standards. That's not pride—that's purity.
- If he can't handle boundaries, he can't handle you.
- Avoid situations that trigger old habits. If you're weak in an area, don't flirt with it.
- Know your value—and don't negotiate it.

Proverbs 4:23 (NLT)
"Guard your heart above all else, for it determines the course of your life."

Loving Again–The Right Way

Before I could truly love someone else, I had to learn to love myself.

I had to learn how to enjoy being alone.
I had to learn how to like my own company.
I had to stop needing someone to validate my worth.
I had to be okay sitting with God and letting Him tell me who I am.

What I'm encouraging you to do is take action on everything mentioned — learning to love and value yourself, and to spend quality time with yourself.

How do you learn how to love yourself? You start by doing for you what you would want someone who truly loves you to do. Think about how you would show love to a future spouse — the care, thoughtfulness, affection, and start practicing that love with yourself.

Love is not just a word. It's an action word. And the same way we show others we care, we must show ourselves that same kindness.

For example, take time to do the little things that make you feel valued and seen. Buy yourself flowers. Take a quiet walk in the park. Read a book that lifts your spirit. Prepare your favorite meal and enjoy it without guilt or rush. Do something that makes you smile. These aren't acts of vanity — they're acts of acknowledgment that say, "I am worth care. I am worth peace. I am worth love."

But it's not just about the physical actions. It's also spiritual. You can love yourself by affirming God's truth over your life — speaking His Word daily. Quote scriptures that remind you of who you are in Christ and what He says about you. Pray, worship, and rest in His presence.

When you take the time to nurture yourself — body, mind, and spirit —you honor the God who created you. You're saying, "Lord, I see the value You've placed in me, and I will take care of what You've made."

Loving yourself also means learning how to be alone and still feel complete. Many people fear solitude, but it's in solitude that God teaches us how to hear Him clearly. It's where He restores us, refreshes us, and reminds us that we were never meant to find completeness in another person — only in Him.

And most importantly, remember that valuing your life means living for God. The greatest act of love was when He sent His only begotten Son to die for our sins so that we could have everlasting life. That alone is proof that you are loved beyond measure — and that you're worth treating with the same care Heaven has already given you.

Building in the Quiet Place

Before the marriage, before the title, before the healing—I had to sit in my quiet and let God rebuild me.

What does that look like?

Sometimes life moves so fast that we forget to be still. Every day brings something new — a new responsibility, a new problem to solve, a new distraction. The world teaches us to keep going, to keep moving, to stay busy. But when I say, I had to sit in my quiet and let God rebuild me, I mean that I had to do the opposite. I had to stop.

That meant literally turning everything off — the phone, the television, the music, even the thoughts that tried to crowd my mind. I had to learn how to slow down and just be. I had to give myself permission to rest in His presence without feeling guilty for it.

Sometimes that quiet place looked like sitting in my favorite prayer chair with my Bible open, but not saying a word. Other times, it looked like sitting in the bathtub with the lights low and letting my thoughts drift toward God. I would breathe, reflect, and allow His peace to settle over me.

In the stillness, I wasn't performing for God. I wasn't praying fancy prayers or trying to sound holy. I was just being with Him. Because when you're still, you start to sense things that you can't hear in the noise. You start to recognize His whisper — His guidance, His comfort, His correction, His love.

Sometimes He would bring a scripture to my mind. Other times, He wouldn't say anything at all. But even in the silence, I could feel His presence. It's like a warm blanket covering your soul. The quiet became the place where I could breathe again — where I could think clearly, heal deeply, and listen to the heart of God without interruption.

Being in my quiet taught me that God doesn't always move in the noise or the rush. Sometimes, He moves in the whisper, in the calm, in the stillness. That's where He rebuilds us — piece by piece, moment by moment.

Scripture Reflection:

"And He said, Go forth, and stand upon the mount before the Lord. And, behold, the Lord passed by, and a great and strong wind rent the mountains, and brake in pieces the rocks before the Lord; but the Lord was not in the wind: and after the wind an earthquake; but the Lord was not in the earthquake: And after the earthquake a fire; but the Lord was not in the fire: and after the fire a still small voice."
— 1 Kings 19:11–12 (KJV)

God's greatest rebuilding work often happens in the quiet places — not in the chaos of the storm, but in the stillness of His voice.

Learning to Love -- Yourself

Now that I know who I am, I don't rush into anything that doesn't reflect my value. And I want you to do the same. Start by loving you. Loving who God created you to be. Because when you love yourself, you won't let anyone mishandle what God made sacred.

Learning how to love myself despite all that I'd done was not easy. It was a process—one that required honesty, patience, and grace. I had to learn how to accept all of me: the good, the bad, and the ugly.

When I talk about change, I talk about acknowledgment. Loving myself meant acknowledging every part of my story—

the things I did wrong, the moments I allowed others to mistreat me, and even the choices I made out of pain. I had to face it all without running from it.

But what I discovered is that the good, the bad, and the ugly do not define me. My value isn't based on my mistakes or my victories—it's based on who God says I am. His love for me isn't conditional; it's covenant.

God doesn't forgive us because we are good. He forgives us because He is good. His Word reminds us in John 3:16 that "God so loved the world that He gave His only begotten Son, that whosoever believeth in Him should not perish, but have everlasting life."

When I finally grasped that truth, everything changed. I realized I am not God—I cannot out-love or out-forgive Him. If the Creator of the universe can forgive me, who am I to hold unforgiveness against myself?

So, to the reader who struggles to move past guilt or shame: if God so loved the world that He gave His only Son, then He also gave you permission to love yourself. Once you repent and receive His forgiveness, you have the authority to forgive yourself and move forward. You can release what held you bound and walk in the same love that set you free.

Your Testimony Is a Weapon

Every single thing I've been through—every mistake, every heartbreak, every bad decision—is now a tool in God's hands.

He gets all of the glory.

Now I can tell someone:

- I know what it's like to be broken.
- I know what it's like to be ashamed.
- I know what it's like to cry after compromise.
- I know what it's like to give away something sacred and want it back.

But I also know what it's like to be restored.

A Season of Restoration

Restoration was one of the hardest but most beautiful parts of my journey. The process of being restored had absolutely nothing to do with my own strength or willpower — it had everything to do with God's will for my life.

At that moment of restoration, I had to completely give up my desires — my plans, my emotions, my expectations — everything I thought I wanted as a woman, as a person, and even as someone who longed for love. I had to surrender it all because everything I had tried to build on my own had already fallen apart. My version of "fixing myself" could only take me so far, but God's restoration reached the parts of me I didn't even know were broken.

Restoration wasn't about me trying harder; it was about me surrendering deeper. It was about letting go of control and saying, "Lord, I can't do this without You." I didn't restore myself — God restored me. And He did it because I finally said yes.

That, yes, changed everything.

When I said yes to God, I didn't realize how big that yes really was. A yes to God is never small — it's not just a personal decision; it's a spiritual declaration. My yes didn't just bring restoration to me; it began to shift the lives of others who were connected to me.

Because when you allow God to restore you, He doesn't just heal your story — He begins to heal the people who were tangled in your story too. My yes to God broke the chain of temptation that connected me to others who were still living in sin. My yes released me, and in doing so, it released others.

That's why your yes to God is so powerful — it's bigger than you. It's bigger than your pain, your past, or your understanding. Your yes is the key that unlocks freedom, not just for yourself but for those watching your transformation.

And that's exactly what happened to me. Once I surrendered and God restored me, people who once knew me as the "old me" began to see a difference. They saw peace where there had been chaos. They saw light where there had been confusion. They saw grace where there had been guilt.

Restoration became my testimony. It became evident that God's power is real.

And when I tell you that I couldn't have done it on my own, I mean that with every fiber of my being. I didn't have the strength to rebuild what sin had destroyed — but God did. He took the pieces of my life and made something whole again, something holy again.

It all began with one word: **yes**.

Scripture Reflection:

"He restoreth my soul: He leadeth me in the paths of righteousness for His name's sake." — Psalm 23:3 (KJV)

True restoration begins when you stop trying to fix yourself and start saying yes to the One who can.

God didn't just clean me up. He gave me favor.
He turned my fragments into fuel. He turned my pain into purpose.
And now I can tell someone else—there is more.

Declaration: Say This with Me

I am not a side piece.
I am not just a piece.
I am God's daughter.
I am restored.
I am set apart.
I am whole.
I am ready for covenant.
I am walking in purpose.
I am His.

Reflection of Chapter Six:

God will take every piece of your broken past and build you a future that brings Him glory. You are not who you used to be. You are not what they said. You are not even what you once believed yourself to be. You are chosen, forgiven, and set apart.

Chapter Six Prayer: A Prayer for Strength and Identity

Father God,

Thank You for Your favor. Thank You for not leaving me in my fragments. Thank You for restoring what was broken and healing what was hurting. I repent for the times I allowed myself to live beneath Your standard, and I thank You for the mercy that met me in my lowest place.

Lord, I declare today that I am Yours. I am no longer bound by my past. I am no longer moved by shame. I walk in purpose. I walk in purity. I walk in wholeness. Help me to guard my heart, to walk in wisdom, and to date with discernment. Help me to set boundaries that protect the temple You gave me.

Let me love myself as You love me. Teach me how to prepare for covenant. Help me to embrace solitude with joy, and community with purpose. Let me walk boldly as the daughter You've called and chosen. Thank You for the favor that followed my fragments.

In Jesus' name,
Amen.

Chapter Seven: Skeletons In the Closet

There's a phrase we all know too well: "Skeletons in the closet."

It's usually whispered. It's often used as a threat.
It's the fear that if the truth gets out, we'll be ruined.
And so we hide.

When I was , surrendering to a man who did not belong to me, I kept everything a secret. I kept those secrets so deep that not even the people closest to me knew what was going on. My family didn't know. My friends didn't know. Even some of the members at my church — people I prayed with, served with, and worshiped beside — had no idea what I was carrying.

I kept it all in.

The truth is, I was ashamed. I was embarrassed. I didn't want anyone to know what I was going through or what I was doing. I didn't want to face the disappointment in people's eyes, and I didn't want to deal with the judgment that I assumed would come if they knew. So instead, I carried it all — the lies, the guilt, the double life — and I kept piling those skeletons into a closet that eventually became too full to hide.

I just tried to manage it all on my own. But as God began to deal with me — reshaping my heart and healing my soul — He started cleaning out that closet.

It didn't happen all at once. Some of the skeletons fell out on their own — through unexpected conversations, through conviction, through people finding out things that I never meant to share. And while that was painful and embarrassing, it was also freeing. I didn't understand at the time that God can't heal what you're trying to hide.

The process of letting the skeletons fall out was part of my restoration. It was part of my deliverance. Every time one fell, it hurt a little — but it also lightened the load.

And now, I can honestly say that this very book — the one you're holding in your hands — is part of that cleansing. It's my open closet. It's my testimony. It's the story of how God took the hidden parts of my life and turned them into a message of hope.

No, I'm not saying that people will never have skeletons in their closets. We all have done things that we're not proud of, things we've kept hidden. But what I am saying is that there's a time and a place when God will call you to release them. He'll tell you when it's time to let those bones fall, not to shame you, but to free you.

And when they fall — when the truth comes out — don't run from it. Embrace it as part of your healing. Because every skeleton that's released makes room for something holy to take its place.

It's the cleansing of my closet. It's proof that God can turn even the most hidden pain into a public testimony for His glory.

Scripture Reflection:

"Therefore confess your faults one to another, and pray one for another, that ye may be healed. The effectual fervent prayer of a righteous man availeth much." —James 5:16 (KJV)

Healing begins when what's hidden is brought into the light — because what's exposed to the light can no longer hold you captive.

We bury our past. We cover our shame.
We convince ourselves, "If people knew what I've done, they'd never respect me again."

But let me tell you something God taught me:
The enemy doesn't want you to hide your skeletons. He wants you to worship them in silence.
Because when you won't talk about what you've overcome, you give it the power to keep you bound.

But what the devil meant for destruction, God meant for glory.

Remember The Skeletons

When I think about how God took the skeletons in my closet and gave me life again, I'm reminded of the story in the book of Ezekiel, where God led the prophet into a valley full of dry bones. Those bones represented death — lifelessness — and the Lord asked Ezekiel a question: "Son of man, can these bones live?"

Ezekiel didn't try to answer out of his own understanding. He said, "O Lord God, Thou knowest." (Ezekiel 37:3).

And that's where the miracle began. God told Ezekiel to prophesy to the bones — to speak life over what had been buried and forgotten. And as Ezekiel obeyed, the bones began to come together, bone to bone. Flesh and skin covered them, and breath entered them, and what was once dead began to live again.

That's what God did for me.

My skeletons were once a valley of dry bones — lifeless, hidden, and without hope. But when God spoke to me, when He told me to share my story and speak life into what was once dead, those bones began to live again. My past — the same past I used to hide — became the testimony that now breathes life into others.

He took what was buried in shame and resurrected it as purpose.

So yes, the skeletons in my closet once represented sin and pain, but now they represent resurrection and redemption. They are proof that nothing is too dead, too lost, or too broken for God to revive.

Just like in Ezekiel's vision, God took what was once dry and empty in me and filled it with His Spirit. Now, instead of hiding those bones, I use them to show others that if God can breathe life into me, He can breathe life into you, too.

Scripture Reflection:

Ezekiel 37:3–6 (KJV) "And He said unto me, Son of man, can these bones live? And I answered, O Lord God, Thou knowest. Again He said unto me, Prophesy upon these bones, and say unto them, O ye dry bones, hear the word of the Lord. Thus saith the Lord God unto these bones; Behold, I will cause breath to enter into you, and ye shall live."

Ezekiel 37:10 (KJV) "So I prophesied as He commanded me, and the breath came into them, and they lived, and stood up upon their feet, an exceeding great army."

Reflection Thought:

When God breathes into the buried places of your life, the very things that once brought you shame can become the greatest testimony of His power.

You're Not the Only One

Maybe you've been the side piece.

Maybe you were the adulterer.

Maybe you were the one who got cheated on, the one who slept with someone's husband, the one who stayed too long in a soul tie, or the one who lived recklessly even while singing in the choir on Sunday.

Maybe you went left when God clearly told you to go right.

Guess what?

You're not the only one. And you won't be the last.

You are not alone. And you are not disqualified.

Transparency Is Not a Weakness–It's a Weapon

One of the enemy's greatest tricks is shame.
He'll whisper things like:

- *"Don't say anything. People will think less of you."*
- *"If you tell the truth, they'll cancel you."*
- *"Your past disqualifies your ministry."*

But that's a lie from the pit of hell.

Because what you've lived through might be the very key to someone else's freedom.

My Story. Their Need.

In my own experience, I've learned that being a witness to others doesn't always mean sitting down to tell my exact story or reliving every detail of what I went through. Sometimes, it simply means letting people know that I've been through something, that I've struggled, and that I know what it feels like to be bound — but I also know what it feels like to be set free.

When I share, I don't have to tell everything that transpired; I just have to tell them what God did. I tell them how His grace found me, how His mercy carried me, and how His power delivered me. I tell them that deliverance wasn't instant — it was a process — but it was possible.

I've learned to use my story to show others that God still delivers. He still heals. He still restores. He still breathes life into what seems dead. My testimony is not about shame — it's about freedom.

And now, I find myself in situations where I might be out somewhere — walking in a store, sitting at a restaurant, or even attending an event — and I'll run into someone from my past. Sometimes it's someone who knew about my old life, or even someone who was connected to it. And instead of feeling fear, guilt, or shame, I smile. Because now, when they see me, they see freedom.

They see evidence that God is real.

Sometimes those encounters open the door to conversation. And even though I don't go into details, I'm able to say, "God brought me through something that I thought would destroy me, but He didn't let it. He turned it around." And that's enough. Because what I've learned is that you don't have to tell every chapter of your story — sometimes just saying, "God did it," is enough to let someone else know that He can do it for them too.

That's the beauty of deliverance — it's not just about being set free. It's about being used by God to help others find their freedom, too.

So, if it's not about telling and being transparent, then why now?

Why share this testimony in this season? Why write this book now, after all these years?

Because the Lord told me it's time.

I believe the reason God allowed me to release this testimony now is because of the state of the world we're living in. Everywhere we turn, we see brokenness — in homes, in marriages, in relationships, and even within the church. There's so much spiritual confusion, and so many people are bound by the same traps that once had me bound.

In the book of Revelation and throughout the Word of God, we're warned about the signs and conditions that will unfold before Christ's return. And if we pay attention, we can see those very things happening now. I believe that God is preparing His people — not to scare us, but to wake us up.

This book, this testimony, is my obedience to that call.

There are men and women all over this world — saved and unsaved — who have accepted being "side pieces" or "just pieces," who are living in situations that are out of alignment with God's will. They've normalized it, glamorized it, and even justified it, just as I once did. But God is calling His people higher. He's calling His daughters and His sons back to holiness, back to wholeness, back to truth.

So, why now?

Because the time is short. Because souls are at stake. Because deliverance is still available, but it must be accepted.

God is allowing me to tell my story now because someone out there is living the same story I once lived, and they don't know how to get out. He's allowing me to be transparent because it will open the door to someone else's transformation.

This book isn't about exposing sin — it's about exposing grace. It's about showing people that there's still time to turn around, still time to be made whole, still time to let God breathe life into what's dying.

I truly believe that — people who are tired of pretending, tired of hiding, tired of living beneath their purpose. He's calling us to repentance, restoration, and readiness.

Because the truth is — time is winding up. And just as God gave me the opportunity to get it right, He's giving others that same opportunity now.

Revelation 12:11 (KJV) "And they overcame him by the blood of the Lamb, and by the word of their testimony..."

Your testimony is a sword in the spirit.

Your voice isn't just for praise—it's for warfare.

God Knew About the Skeletons Before You Tried to Hide Them

We act as if we don't say it, God won't see it.

But God saw it all. He was there in the darkest nights.
He knew you were going to mess up. And He loved you anyway.

Psalm 139:1–3 (NIV) "You have searched me, Lord, and you know me. You know when I sit and when I rise...you are familiar with all my ways."

You don't have to hide from a God who already knows.

You don't have to pretend for a Savior who already died for it.

If God has forgiven it, healed it, and restored you from it, then it no longer has the power to shame you.

He'll Use What You've Been Through to Help Others Through

Some of the most powerful ministries I've ever witnessed didn't come from people with perfect records. It came from women who said:

- "Yes, I was the other woman."
- "Yes, I slept around."
- "Yes, I knew better and still did wrong."
- "Yes, I had to crawl out of my shame."

And then they said:

- "But God forgave me."
- "God loved me."
- "God still called me."

Romans 8:28 (NIV) "And we know that in all things God works for the good of those who love Him, who have been called according to His purpose."

Everything you went through—the sin, the heartbreak, the secret, the shame—can be used for a purpose.

Your voice brings Him glory.

From Skeletons to Sanctuary

God has a way of turning the very thing that was hidden in the closet into the very thing He builds a ministry platform upon.

With the skeletons that were once in my closet, the Lord has allowed me to see how He can take what was once my greatest shame and turn it into one of my strongest testimonies. What was once buried and hidden, He has now used as a foundation — a platform that declares His grace, His mercy, and His power to redeem.

This platform isn't about me or about boasting in what I've done. It's about boasting in the Lord — the One who took the broken pieces of my life and built something beautiful out of them. He allowed me to openly share my story, not for attention or pity, but as a living example of what His forgiveness looks like in action.

God took my pain and gave it purpose.
He took my shame and gave it strength.
He took my silence and gave it a sound.

And now, that sound is the testimony I carry — one that helps set others free.

By telling my story, I'm not glorifying the mistakes; I'm glorifying the Maker who brought me out. And in doing so, He's shown me that I can speak boldly because Christ lives in me. That boldness doesn't come from confidence in myself; it comes from confidence in Him.

My story is not just my own — it's a message to every woman and every man who has been in bondage, who has been ashamed, who has hidden their pain in silence. It's to let them know that God can free you, too. That He can take your story — yes, even the messy parts — and turn it into a ministry that reaches others.

Because what God delivers you from, He can also use you to deliver others through.

My Story. His Glory.

What was once a skeleton becomes a stone in your testimony altar. You thought that thing would ruin you? Watch God use it to rebuild you.

You thought no one would love you if they found out? Watch God surround you with people who only love you more because you were honest enough to be healed.

Speak, Even If Your Voice Shakes

You don't have to tell everything to everybody.
But you do have to be willing to use your story for God's glory.

Using my story is definitely bigger than myself. I've come to realize that during the process of God healing and delivering me, He was also preparing me to fall into His arms and allow Him to use me according to His will. Part of that use is helping people understand that the story I tell—the testimony I give, the life experiences I share—are never meant to glorify me. They are meant to glorify Him.

When God truly changes you, He teaches you what it means to become selfless. My life is no longer my own. Every word I speak, every page I write, and every opportunity I'm given to testify is for His glory alone.

When we say "yes" to God, that yes is so much bigger than we realize. It's not just a personal yes—it's a yes that creates ripples in the Spirit. It's a yes that unlocks deliverance for others. It's a yes that opens the door to healing, salvation, and freedom to flow into other lives.

My "yes" became a domino effect. By surrendering to God, I gave Him permission to use my life as an example that He can do anything with anyone who's willing to let Him. It's never been about my strength—it's about His strength working through me.

One of my favorite scriptures reminds me of this daily:

"I can do all things through Christ which strengtheneth me."
— Philippians 4:13 (KJV)

That verse is more than words on a page—it's my reality. It's the reason I can tell this story without shame or fear. Because every time I speak, write, or share, I do it through His strength.

And I hold firmly to the promise of Romans 8:28:

"And we know that all things work together for good to them that love God, to them who are called according to his purpose."

Everything—my mistakes, my tears, my healing, my testimony—has worked together for His good. So, whatever I do, I'll continue to do it for the glory of God.

Reflection Thought:

When you surrender your story to God, He multiplies your yes. One act of obedience is worth more than one thousand sacrifices.

Because somewhere, another woman is feeling:

- Ashamed of her past
- Embarrassed by her current struggle
- Unworthy of love
- Too broken to be used by God

And your voice might be the very thing that tells her:

"You're not alone—and this doesn't have to be the end of your story."

Reflection of Chapter Seven:

The voice the enemy tried to silence is the same voice God will use to deliver others. You don't have to be perfect to be powerful. You just have to be honest.

Declaration: Say This With Me

My voice is not a weapon of shame.
My story is sacred.
My past is under the blood.
My testimony is powerful.
My identity is secure.
I am no longer afraid.
I will speak, and God will get the glory.

Chapter Seven Prayer: A Prayer For Boldness and Freedom

Father God,

Thank You for knowing me completely—and loving me anyway. Thank You for covering me in grace when I was wrapped in shame. Thank You for forgiving the parts of my past I was too afraid to speak aloud. Lord, I give You every skeleton, every secret, every shameful moment. Use it for Your glory. Use it to help someone else. I silence the voice of the accuser, and I lift my voice as a testimony of Your power.

Help me to speak with boldness, live with transparency, and walk in freedom. May my voice deliver the hurting, restore the broken, and glorify Your name. Let me never be afraid to tell the truth—because You already know it and You've already redeemed it.

In Jesus' name,
Amen.

Chapter Eight: Becoming a Covenant Keeper

Deliverance is a moment, but discipline is a lifestyle. Discipline is definitely a way of life for me. Going through the change and allowing God to transform me wasn't something that happened overnight. It took an intentional process of letting Him change my thoughts, my habits, and my heart. Renewal didn't just come through a single moment of deliverance — it came through consistency in His Word and commitment to His presence.

For me, discipline meant learning to "kill the flesh" daily. Every day, I had to make a choice: either feed my spirit or feed my flesh. I had to guard what I allowed into my mind, what I listened to, and who I surrounded myself with. I had to stay away from anything that would tempt me to go backward. Discipline meant saying no to things that once had me bound and yes to the things that would keep me spiritually free.

One way I built that discipline was through my prayer journal. Even when I wasn't speaking aloud to God, I was writing to Him. I poured my heart into my prayer journals — the pain, the struggle, the gratitude, the repentance, the praise. Over the years, I have filled many journals, and every now and then, I go back and read them. They remind me of how far God has brought me and how faithful He has been. They're not just memories; they're monuments of deliverance.

Discipline is also about spiritual exercise. Just as someone trying to lose weight must commit to physical fitness — walking daily, eating well, and maintaining a routine — our spiritual health requires the same level of intentionality. I had to keep feeding myself the Word of God, set and keep boundaries, and not break them when temptation came.

I learned that I couldn't rely on my own strength. My yes to God had to be an active yes — not just a verbal one. So, I allowed my yes to be yes and my no to be no, even when it was hard. And that consistency became a lifestyle.

Today, discipline for me includes daily prayer, consistent Bible reading, and fasting. The Bible says, *"Howbeit this kind goeth not out but by prayer and fasting" (Matthew 17:21)*. Some strongholds break only when you fast — when you turn down your plate and focus on feeding your spirit instead of your flesh. Fasting humbles the body, allowing the spirit to be strengthened.

Discipline keeps me grounded. It keeps me rooted in the things of God and helps me maintain the freedom that He gave me. It's not about perfection — it's about persistence.

It's one thing to say "I'm no longer that woman," but it's another thing to live that out daily. Becoming a covenant keeper means walking in intentional holiness — not just in your marriage, but in your heart, mind, choices, and character.

Be a Covenant Keeper

How do we do that? How do we walk in covenant not only with our spouse but with God — in our heart, our mind, our choices, and our character?

It starts with surrender. When you truly surrender to God's will, you're not just asking Him to bless your life; you're giving Him permission to transform your life. You're allowing Him to come into every hidden place — into the heart, the mind, the thoughts, and the emotions — and make them new.

When I prayed and asked God to change my heart and renew my mind, it wasn't easy. It was a spiritual crushing. (Can we stop right here for one moment. This is a great place for you to be BOLD in your prayers, asking God to change your heart and renew your mind. Let the spiritual crushing commence.) The Lord began to strip away everything in me that didn't look like Him. It wasn't just a gentle pruning — it was a full breaking and reshaping.

That crushing process is painful. It's painful because it means letting go of people, habits, and thoughts that once felt comfortable. It's painful because your flesh begins to yearn for what your spirit is starving for. But the beauty of that process is that it leads to freedom.

When you intentionally walk in holiness — when you choose to live in covenant with God — it means you're allowing Him to renew not just your behavior but your being. You're inviting Him to sanctify your character, your mindset, and your daily choices.

Intentional holiness means being conscious of what you say, how you think, and how you respond. It means recognizing that your body is a temple of the Holy Spirit and that your heart, mind, and spirit must remain aligned with the Word of God.

And it's not by our strength that we do this. It's never by our own willpower. It's by His strength. Because when we surrender, He empowers us. He gives us the grace to live right, the courage to stand firm, and the peace that keeps us steady.

As the Apostle Paul wrote in Romans 12:2, "*Be not conformed to this world, but be ye transformed by the renewing of your mind.*" Transformation is not a one-time event — it's a daily commitment to walk in covenant with God.

Scripture Reflection:

"Create in me a clean heart, O God; and renew a right spirit within me." — Psalm 51:10 (KJV)
"Be not conformed to this world: but be ye transformed by the renewing of your mind." — Romans 12:2 (KJV)
"He must increase, but I must decrease." — John 3:30 (KJV)

Reflection Thought:

The crushing is not meant to destroy you — it's meant to transform you. When the flesh dies, the spirit thrives.

The Temptations - Not the Singers

There are temptations. There are triggers. There are things you've been delivered from that will try to call you back.

But God has given you power, tools, and the Holy Ghost to stay free.

The power that He's given us is His strength — the same resurrection power that raised Jesus from the dead now lives inside of us. It's not our own willpower or determination that keeps us free; it's the power of Christ Jesus working within us. That power gives us authority over temptation, over the enemy, and over the things that once held us captive.

When Christ lives on the inside of us, His power transfers into our spirit. Philippians 4:13 reminds us, "*I can do all things through Christ which strengtheneth me.*" That strength doesn't come from self-discipline alone — it comes from divine empowerment.

There are other scriptures that remind us of this power:

"But ye shall receive power, after that the Holy Ghost is come upon you." —Acts 1:8
"Behold, I give unto you power to tread on serpents and scorpions, and over all the power of the enemy." — Luke 10:19
"Greater is He that is in you, than he that is in the world." — 1 John 4:4

These verses show us that we are not powerless. We are equipped.

And the tools God has given us are what keep that power active. The first and greatest tool is His Word — the Holy Bible. The Word of God feeds our spirit, renews our mind, and gives us divine direction. It is our sword in spiritual warfare. Ephesians 6:17 calls it "*the sword of the Spirit, which is the Word of God.*"

Another essential tool is prayer. Prayer connects us to Heaven's strength and keeps our spiritual communication line open. Through prayer, we gain revelation, endurance, and peace.

God also provides us with the Holy Spirit — our Comforter and our Guide. The Holy Spirit convicts, teaches, and comforts us, keeping us aligned with God's will. He is the inner witness that whispers truth when the world speaks confusion.

And finally, God gives us the church — a spiritual home and a community of believers. Being planted in a healthy church allows us to grow, to be nurtured, and to be held accountable. Iron sharpens iron, and fellowship strengthens faith.

All of these — the power, the Word, prayer, the Holy Spirit, and the church community — work together to help us stay free. Deliverance gets us out, but these tools keep us out.

Scripture Reflection:

"For the weapons of our warfare are not carnal, but mighty through God to the pulling down of strongholds." — 2 Corinthians 10:4

"Thy word is a lamp unto my feet, and a light unto my path." — Psalm 119:105

"Pray without ceasing." — 1 Thessalonians 5:17

Reflection Thought:

Power keeps you strong; the tools keep you steady. When you stay rooted in the Word, in prayer, and in the Spirit, you won't just get free — you'll stay free.

Detoxing from Ungodly Attachments

Before you can maintain a covenant, you must detox from what once kept you bound.

Detoxing — spiritual detoxification — is an essential part of staying free. For me, detox meant replacing what I used to do with things that glorify God. It meant no longer feeding my spirit with the same toxins that once poisoned me.

One of the spiritual addictions that attached itself to me had to be broken through detox. When temptation tried to rise up, I had to make a choice. There were times when I had to literally run. Just like Joseph in the Bible (Genesis 39:12) ran from Potiphar's wife when she tried to tempt him, sometimes you have to physically remove yourself from situations that could pull you back into bondage.

That's what spiritual detox looks like — removing yourself from people, places, or things that awaken the flesh instead of the spirit.

The Word of God reminds us that with every temptation, "God is faithful, who will not suffer you to be tempted above that ye are able; but will with the temptation also make a way to escape" (1 Corinthians 10:13). That "way of escape" is your detox.

There were times when my detox meant turning off the television when inappropriate scenes came on. Other times, it meant turning on TBN or listening to gospel music instead of secular songs that stirred up my emotions. Sometimes it meant closing my phone, deleting a number, or cutting off communication altogether.

Detox also means learning how to replace those sinful thoughts with the Word of God. When the enemy whispers lies, you replace them with truth. You speak God's Word out loud. You declare it until your mind agrees with your spirit.

You might have to say:

- "I am the righteousness of God through Christ Jesus" (2 Corinthians 5:21).
- "I am fearfully and wonderfully made" (Psalm 139:14).
- "I am more than a conqueror through Him who loves me" (Romans 8:37).

Detoxing is also spiritual warfare. The enemy doesn't fight fairly, and he doesn't tempt you with what you don't like. He tempts you with what your flesh craves. But once you recognize his patterns, you take back your power through the Word.

The Bible says, "*Resist the devil, and he will flee from you*" (James 4:7). Sometimes resisting means literally walking away. Sometimes it means declaring God's Word. And sometimes it means crying out in prayer and saying, "Lord, help me!"

Whatever it takes, run from sin. Rebuke it. Denounce it. And don't be ashamed to speak to that thing that once had you bound. Because through Christ, you have authority to speak to mountains and command them to move (Mark 11:23).

Spiritual detox isn't easy — but it's necessary. And once you go through it, you'll find that what once tempted you no longer has power over you.

Even Jesus Himself showed us what true spiritual detox and discipline look like. After fasting for forty days and forty nights in the wilderness, He was tempted three times by the devil (Matthew 4:1–11).

The enemy came at Him when His flesh was at its weakest, when He was hungry and physically worn. But instead of giving in, Jesus fought back with the Word of God.

When the devil said, "*If you are the Son of God, command these stones to be made bread,*" Jesus responded, "*It is written, Man shall not live by bread alone, but by every word that proceedeth out of the mouth of God.*" *(Matthew 4:4)*

When Satan tried again, tempting Him to throw Himself down from the temple to test God's protection, Jesus replied, "*It is written again, Thou shalt not tempt the Lord thy God.*" *(Matthew 4:7)*

And when the devil made one last attempt — offering Him all the kingdoms of the world if Jesus would bow down and worship him — Jesus rebuked him with authority: "Get thee hence, Satan: for it is written, Thou shalt worship the Lord thy God, and Him only shalt thou serve." (Matthew 4:10)

Three Temptations. Three Responses. Every Single One With Scripture.

That's the pattern for spiritual detox — not relying on emotion, but responding with truth. Jesus didn't argue, He didn't rationalize, and He didn't entertain the enemy. He spoke the Word, and the Word had power.

When we're tempted, the same strategy applies. Speak the Word of God. Declare what He says over your life. Rebuke the lies of the enemy and replace them with the promises of Scripture. That's how you starve your flesh and strengthen your spirit.

And just like with Jesus, when you resist the enemy with the Word, the Bible says, "*Then the devil leaveth Him, and behold, angels came and ministered unto Him." (Matthew 4:11)*

That's what happens when you detox — when you stand firm and resist. The devil flees, and God sends peace, restoration, and strength to refresh your spirit.

Scripture Reflection:

"Then was Jesus led up of the Spirit into the wilderness to be tempted of the devil." — Matthew 4:1 (KJV)
"It is written, Man shall not live by bread alone, but by every word that proceedeth out of the mouth of God." — Matthew 4:4 (KJV)
"Submit yourselves therefore to God. Resist the devil, and he will flee from you." — James 4:7 (KJV)

Reflection Thought:

When temptation comes, don't wrestle with it — speak to it. The Word of God is your weapon, and every time you declare it, the enemy loses his grip.

Addicted to Sin

Some sins are not just mistakes — they become addictions. Emotional addictions. Sexual addictions. Soul ties. Toxic conversations. Destructive habits. You can't enter covenant still tasting poison from the last season.

2 Corinthians 6:17 (KJV) "Wherefore come out from among them, and be ye separate, saith the Lord, and touch not the unclean thing; and I will receive you."

When you detox spiritually, you start:

- Letting go of people God told you to leave.
- Cutting the secret strings of lust and fantasy.
- Refusing to romanticize your former life.
- Rejecting anything that invites those old spirits back in.

You cannot live holy while holding onto hell's souvenirs.

Breaking the Addiction to Sin

Addiction is not just about substances — it's about cravings. Sin feeds the flesh and makes the spirit starve. When you're addicted to the feelings sin gives you (attention, control, orgasm, escape, emotional highs), you start craving what God never intended for your spiritual diet.

Those addictions I'm talking about aren't just emotional—they're spiritual. For me, one of the hardest chains to break was sexual addiction.

It started subtly. What I thought was just "pleasing the person I was with" slowly became pleasing the cravings of my flesh. The more I entertained those desires, the stronger they grew. What started with sex outside of marriage opened the door to pornography. And pornography opened the door to sex toys and a deeper desire to fulfill lust rather than love.

At first, I convinced myself it was harmless—just a way to learn or explore—but the truth is, I was feeding the very thing that was destroying me spiritually. The more I fed my flesh, the weaker my spirit became.

Before long, I realized that even when I wasn't with the person I had been involved with, I was still craving those images, those thoughts, those feelings. That's when I knew it had become an addiction. It wasn't about love or connection anymore—it was bondage.

I remember thinking that as long as I wasn't physically with anyone, I was okay. But the Holy Spirit convicted me and reminded me that sin doesn't always require a partner; it just needs participation. The Bible says in Romans 1:26–27 and 1 Corinthians 6:18–20 that our bodies are temples of the Holy Spirit, and that sexual sin is a sin against our own body.

It was easier for me to stop using the toys, but breaking free from pornography was a battle. It lingered long after I walked away from being a side piece, because pornography is not just visual—it's spiritual. It rewires your mind, desensitizes your heart, and makes your spirit sick.

There were nights I cried out to God, saying, "Lord, I don't want this anymore!" There were times when I would fast, pray, and read His Word just to silence the thoughts that tried to return. And every time I resisted, I could feel God making me stronger.

One day, something shifted. I woke up and realized the desire was gone. Completely gone. The thought of it disgusted me. The same thing that once tempted me now turned my stomach. That's when I knew God had truly delivered me—not because I was strong, but because He was.

When God delivers you, He doesn't just cover the sin—He cleans it out. He removes the taste, the desire, and the appetite. But you must be willing. You must let Him.

Even now, the enemy will try to bring back old memories or flash images from my past to tempt me again, but I remind him of my victory in Christ. I remind him that I am delivered. And every time he tries to whisper, I speak the Word of God aloud:

"Whom the Son sets free is free indeed." —John 8:36

So, when we talk about addictions, this is what it looked like for me. It was an ongoing battle, but I learned that God doesn't just want to deliver us from sin—He wants to detox us from the aftereffects of sin. Because when you are spiritually detoxed, the things that once controlled you lose their power.

Scripture Reflection:

"Flee from sexual immorality... Do you not know that your bodies are temples of the Holy Spirit?" — 1 Corinthians 6:18–19 (NIV)
"Whom the Son sets free is free indeed." —John 8:36 (KJV)
"Blessed are the pure in heart, for they shall see God." — Matthew 5:8 (KJV)

Reflection Thought:

Deliverance breaks the chains, but detox drains the residue. God doesn't just take you out of sin—He takes the sin out of you.

The Truth About Sin

But here's the truth:
The same way you trained yourself to depend on sin is the same way you can retrain yourself to depend on God.

Romans 13:14 (NIV) "Clothe yourselves with the Lord Jesus Christ, and do not think about how to gratify the desires of the flesh."

Fasting. Prayer. Worship. Accountability.
These are your new cravings. Replace the appetite for lust with an appetite for the presence of God.

Feeding the Spirit, Not the Flesh

Galatians 5:16 (KJV) "Walk in the Spirit, and ye shall not fulfil the lust of the flesh."

The flesh doesn't just go away after you get saved.
It just doesn't get to sit in the driver's seat anymore.

You feed what you focus on:

- If you feed your lust, your lust will grow.
- If you feed your spirit, your spirit will lead.

Let the Word of God become your food:

- Daily devotions
- Scripture memorization
- Christian community and teaching
- Spirit-led journaling and reflection

Covenant Requires Accountability

You can't live holy in isolation. You need safe people who will help you stay aligned.

- Women who aren't afraid to say, "That's not of God."
- Marriage mentors who speak life into your relationship.
- Prayer partners who war with you when you're weak.
- Spiritual leaders who don't flatter your flesh but correct your walk.

Ecclesiastes 4:9–10 (NIV) "Two are better than one... If either of them falls down, one can help the other up."

Accountability isn't about control — it's about covenant protection.

The Holy Spirit Will Warn You – Listen

Some call it intuition. But what you're sensing is not from the mind — it's from the Holy Spirit. There is a difference between intuition and having discernment.

For me, that difference became clear through experience.

When I was trying to break free from being a side piece on my own strength, my intuition told me I could still be connected to the person as long as I wasn't sleeping with him. I convinced myself that we could be "just friends." I told myself that I could still talk to him, still check in, and still keep him in my life because, in my mind, I wasn't sinning anymore — I just wasn't cutting ties.

Intuition told me that I might need him one day. Intuition told me that because he was a "good person" or "a good friend," it was okay to stay connected. But discernment — true, godly discernment — revealed something different.

Discernment showed me that as long as I stayed connected to him in any way, I was still bound. Even if I wasn't physically involved, I was still spiritually entangled. And that's the trick of the enemy — to make us believe that as long as we stop "doing the act," the soul tie is broken. But sometimes, the connection is emotional, and it's just as powerful as the physical one.

Discernment taught me that no matter how harmless it looked, I was still holding onto something that wasn't mine. And as long as I stayed connected to that person, I was still leaving a door open for the enemy to creep back in.

When I finally began to rely on God's strength and not my own, discernment replaced my intuition. I stopped listening to my emotions, and I started listening to the Holy Spirit. Discernment showed me that, even though the conversations seemed friendly, they were rooted in something toxic, something born of sin.

Discernment showed me that in order for God to use me fully, I had to cut all ties completely. There could be no "just checking in," no "friendly text," no "remember when." Nothing. Because anything built outside of God's will has to be dismantled for new things to grow.

And once I finally let go — once I truly cut off all contact — I felt free. It was like a spiritual chain had been broken. I realized that while my intuition wanted to maintain control, my discernment called me to surrender.

That's the difference between the two.

Intuition is based on feeling.

Discernment is based on Spirit.

- Intuition will have you doing what feels safe.

- Discernment will have you doing what is right in God's eyes.

And when you choose discernment, you choose freedom.

Scripture Reflection:

"Trust in the Lord with all thine heart; and lean not unto thine own understanding. In all thy ways acknowledge Him, and He shall direct thy paths." — Proverbs 3:5–6 (KJV)

"But solid food belongs to those who are of full age, that is, those who by reason of use have their senses exercised to discern both good and evil." — Hebrews 5:14 (NKJV)

"Do not be unequally yoked together with unbelievers. For what fellowship has righteousness with lawlessness? And what communion has light with darkness?" — 2 Corinthians 6:14 (NKJV)

Reflection Thought:

Discernment will always lead you closer to God, while intuition will often lead you back to yourself. True freedom comes when you stop trusting your feelings and start trusting His voice.

Let's break it down:

Intuition	**Discernment**
• Comes from the soul (mind/will/emotion)	• Comes from the Spirit of God
• Often shaped by personal experiences	• Rooted in divine truth and righteousness
• Can be wrong, based on trauma or bias	• Is accurate when aligned with God's Word
• Causes suspicion	• Reveals truth with wisdom

Discernment will tell you:

- *"This man isn't from God."*
- *"This conversation is seductive."*
- *"This situation is setting you up for a fall."*
- *"Get out. This is familiar territory that once trapped you."*

And if you listen, you'll stay free.

John 16:13 (NIV) "But when He, the Spirit of truth, comes, He will guide you into all the truth..."

Daily Covenant Living

Being a covenant keeper means:

- Waking up daily and choosing God again.

- Checking your thoughts before they become actions.
- Surrendering your body, your mouth, your attitude, and your emotions.
- Respecting your marriage as a sacred commitment, not just a title.
- Keeping your vows even when it's not convenient.
- Living holy when no one is watching.

Lamentations 3:22–23 (ESV) "The steadfast love of the Lord never ceases; His mercies never come to an end; they are new every morning..."

Holiness is a daily discipline.
It's not perfection — it's consistency, powered by grace and guarded by love.

Reflection of Chapter Eight:

God doesn't just want you delivered — He wants you disciplined. You are no longer a slave to sin. You are a keeper of the covenant, sealed by the Holy Spirit and empowered to live holy.

Declaration: Say This With Me

I am a covenant keeper.
I walk in the Spirit.
I will not gratify the desires of the flesh.
I release every ungodly tie.
I replace sin with the presence of God.
I am surrounded by truth-tellers.
I am disciplined, not just delivered.
I am kept by grace, and I live by choice.
I belong to God.

Chapter Eight Prayer: A Prayer for Holiness and Strength

Father God,

I thank You for delivering me, but now I ask You to teach me discipline. Help me to walk holy every day. Teach me how to guard my eyes, my ears, my body, and my mind. Detox my spirit from every addiction to sin. Break every ungodly craving and replace it with Your presence.

Let Your Word be my food, Your Spirit my guide, and Your love my foundation. Help me to recognize the difference between intuition and discernment. Give me a discerning heart that knows when something is not of You. Surround me with godly people who will sharpen me and hold me accountable.

And most of all, help me to keep covenant — with You first, with my marriage, and with myself. I am Yours, and I want to live in a way that brings You glory.

In Jesus' name,
Amen.

Chapter Nine: Don't Go Back - Avoiding Spiritual Relapse

There comes a point after deliverance where the real war begins. The enemy doesn't mind that you got free. What scares him is that you might stay free.

Staying free became my next battleground. The enemy knew my patterns, my preferences, my weak places—and he tried to lure me back with the very bait my flesh used to crave. I said, "I'm done," but I said it in my strength. I changed my cell number and felt proud of my progress. But I left one door unlocked—my house phone. When it rang and his name flashed on the caller ID, my flesh tingled. And just like that, I relapsed.

That call taught me something important in deliverance class: freedom isn't just chopping off the stem; it's ripping out the root. If the root stays, it sprouts again. The enemy will test whether you've truly closed every door or merely shut the most obvious one. He doesn't mind if you get free. He panics when you stay free.

So, I learned to close all entries—outer and inner. Not just the number in my phone, but the number in my heart. Not just the places I went, but the reasons I wanted to go. Not just the habits, but the hunger that fed them.

How I pulled the root (and how you can, too):

- Cut every tie, not just the convenient ones. Numbers, socials, mutual "*check-in" threads—gone. "Give no place to the devil.*" (Ephesians 4:27)

- Replace the reflex. When I felt the urge to reach out, I reached up. Prayer, a worship playlist, a Scripture out loud. "*Resist the devil, and he will flee.*" (James 4:7)

- Lock down access. Caller blocks, content filters, quiet hours on devices. This isn't fear; it's wisdom. "*If your right hand causes you to sin, cut it off.*" (Matthew 5:30, paraphrase)

- Tell on yourself to hold accountability. I texted my safe person, "I'm tempted. Call me." Isolation grows relapse; light withers it. "*Two are better than one.*" (Ecclesiastes 4:9–10)

- Fast when the pull feels strong. When appetite bows, the spirit stands taller. "*This kind goeth not out but by prayer and fasting.*" (Matthew 17:21 KJV)

- Guard the gates. Eyes, ears, conversations, places. "Above all else, guard your heart." (Proverbs 4:23 NIV)

Relapse humbled me, but it also healed me—because I stopped boasting in my willpower and started leaning on God's. I learned that real repentance isn't, "I can manage this line," but, "Lord, redraw my map." Staying free required a new internal setting: no more negotiations with what nailed Jesus to the cross.

Scripture anchors for staying free:

- *"Stand fast therefore in the liberty wherewith Christ hath made us free." — Galatians 5:1*
- *"Flee also youthful lusts: but follow righteousness, faith, charity, peace." — 2 Timothy 2:22*
- *"Catch for us the little foxes that ruin the vineyards." — Song of Solomon 2:15 (NIV)*
- *"Each person is tempted when they are dragged away by their own desire... and sin, when it is full-grown, gives birth to death." — James 1:14–15 (paraphrase)*
- *"God... will also make a way to escape." — 1 Corinthians 10:13*

The Enemy Has Returned

After you've been healed, restored, forgiven, and realigned — the enemy will circle back and whisper, "But remember how that used to feel?"

What I've learned is that he doesn't just whisper once. He waits until he thinks your guard is down—when you're tired, distracted, or relaxed—and then he creeps in quietly. For me, it even happened in my sleep.

Shortly after I broke away from that relationship, I began having vivid dreams about the person I had separated from. They felt so real that I would wake up as if I had been intimate, again. I'm being transparent here because somebody reading this has experienced the same thing and wondered what it meant. Those dreams were the enemy's way of taunting me, trying to pull me back into bondage by stirring up what God had already delivered me from.

That's why it's vital to stay prayed up—not just in the morning but throughout the day, and especially before you go to bed. Nighttime can be a battleground if you're not covered. When I finally started praying intentionally over my sleep, asking God to guard my mind and close every open door, the torment stopped.

I realized that the enemy was angry because I had chosen to disconnect completely. He wanted to tempt me through memory and imagination. But the moment I said, "Enough is enough," and let God have total control, those dreams stopped. I no longer woke up feeling violated or disgusted. I woke up in peace.

Temptation doesn't always come with a phone call or a visit. Sometimes it comes through a dream, a memory, or a passing thought. But even there, God gives us authority. We can pray and declare protection over our minds, our bodies, and our rest.

Scripture Reflections

"When you lie down, you will not be afraid; when you lie down, your sleep will be sweet." — Proverbs 3:24

"You will keep in perfect peace those whose minds are stayed on you." — Isaiah 26:3

"Take every thought captive to make it obedient to Christ." — 2 Corinthians 10:5

Reflection Thought:

Even in your dreams, the Holy Spirit can stand guard. When you cover your mind with prayer, no whisper of the enemy can linger where God's peace dwells.

He knows that one emotional moment, one weak day, one forgotten prayer life, one distracted season can send you back into what God pulled you out of.

But the truth is: you don't have to go back.

The Enemy Loves Familiar Territory

The devil doesn't change his tricks — he just waits for you to get tired, complacent, or spiritually dry.

He'll wait until:

- You're lonely.
- You're not praying like you used to.
- You've been disconnected from the community.
- You're too busy to read the Word.

And then he'll bring something familiar back into your life — not because it's new, but because it once worked.

When the enemy brought that person back into my life, it wasn't really about the person — it was about the words. The words were familiar. They were the same sweet conversations that used to pull me in before. "I miss you." "I love you." "You're the only one who understands me." Those words were like bait to my emotions.

At that time, I was still vulnerable. My healing was still fresh, and I hadn't fully learned how to guard my heart. So, when he called and said the same things that used to make my heart melt, my emotions recognized the sound. It was familiar. My flesh remembered it, and that's all the enemy needed — something familiar.

That's how temptation works. The devil rarely shows up with something brand new. He simply replays what worked before. He knows what tone, what scent, what voice, what song, what number to call — and he uses it. Because it's familiar.

And when I listened — when I picked up the phone and listened to those same lies, the same flattery, the same empty promises — I was inviting that spirit back in. I was giving permission for the enemy to rebuild what God had torn down.

Jesus said in Matthew 12:43–45 that when an unclean spirit leaves a person, it wanders for a while and then returns to see if the house is still empty. If it finds that the house has not been filled with the Spirit of God, it comes back with seven more spirits worse than before. That's what happened to me spiritually. When the enemy came back, he came back stronger, and I fell harder.

I noticed it right away. The temptations were heavier. The desire to watch pornography was stronger. The thoughts were darker. The cravings for what God had already freed me from came back with more force, because the door had been cracked open again.

That's why I tell people: be careful what doors you leave open. Be careful what you allow your ears to hear and your emotions to feel. The devil doesn't care if he can't get your body — if he can get your attention, he's already halfway there.

Scripture Reflection

"Above all else, guard your heart, for everything you do flows from it." — Proverbs 4:23

"The thief comes only to steal and kill and destroy; I came that they may have life and have it abundantly." — John 10:10

"When an impure spirit comes out of a person, it goes through arid places seeking rest... then it says, 'I will return to the house I left.'" — Matthew 12:43–45

Reflection Thought:

The enemy will always reuse what once worked. But when you fill your house with the Word, prayer, and worship, there's no room left for him to return.

Luke 11:24–26 (NIV) "When an impure spirit comes out of a person, it goes through arid places seeking rest and does not find it. Then it says, 'I will return to the house I left.'"

Don't leave your spiritual door unlocked.
Your soul must be filled, sealed, and fortified.
This is why you cannot afford to play with deliverance.

Fasting Is Not a Trend – It's a Weapon

We live in a culture where people call everything a "fast."

- No social media?
- No Netflix?
- No sweets?

That's called self-control. Not fasting.

True biblical fasting is the denial of food — something your body needs to survive — to strengthen your spirit man.

For me, fasting was its own process. Just as deliverance, change, and forgiveness had to become learned disciplines, so too did fasting. When I first began, I didn't jump straight into a three-day or seven-day fast—I started small.

I remember telling the Lord, "I want these yokes of my past broken. I want every ungodly tie, every emotional chain, every weight that's been holding me down to be destroyed." That desire led me to fast. I had read in the Word that some things come out only through prayer and fasting (Matthew 17:21), and I knew I needed more than prayer alone.

At first, I could only fast for four or five hours a day. I would pray, read Scripture, and meditate while at work, all while taking care of my children and everyday responsibilities. I had to fast right in the middle of my real life. After those hours, I'd break the fast with something light to eat.

Over time, four hours became eight hours. Eight hours became a full day. And eventually, a full day became two. It wasn't about perfection—it was about consistency. Each time I fasted, I could feel my spirit getting stronger. I started seeing things more clearly, hearing God more clearly, and feeling peace settle in places where confusion used to live.

During those fasts, I surrounded myself with God's presence: worship music, TBN sermons, my Bible, and quiet time with the Lord. I wasn't starving myself—I was feeding my spirit.

That's when I began to understand Isaiah 58 in a new way: fasting isn't about punishment or deprivation; it's about breaking chains, lifting burdens, and letting light break forth in your soul. Fasting gave me the clarity and strength I needed to walk away from the old and stand firm in the new.

Scripture Reflections

"Is not this the fast that I have chosen: to loose the bands of wickedness, to undo the heavy burdens, and to let the oppressed go free?" — Isaiah 58:6
"However, this kind does not go out except by prayer and fasting." — Matthew 17:21 (KJV)
When you fast, anoint your head and wash your face... and your Father who sees in secret will reward you openly." — Matthew 6:17–18

Reflection Thought:

Fasting isn't about what you stop eating—it's about what starts living inside you. When you turn down your plate, heaven turns up its power.

Isaiah 58:6 (KJV) "Is not this the fast that I have chosen? to loose the bands of wickedness, to undo the heavy burdens, and to let the oppressed go free, and that ye break every yoke?"

When you fast from food and feed your soul with prayer and the Word, your flesh becomes weak — and your spirit becomes dominant.

It's during fasting that:

- Lust loses its grip.
- Soul ties are broken.
- The taste for sin fades.
- The spirit becomes sharp and discerning.

Hydrate Your Spirit with the Word

While fasting weakens the flesh, it cannot be complete without feeding your spirit.

The Bible is not optional. It's your daily bread.

Matthew 4:4 (KJV) "Man shall not live by bread alone, but by every word that proceedeth out of the mouth of God."

Hydrate your spirit by:

- Reading Scripture daily (even one chapter).
- Meditating on the Word — not just reading, but studying.
- Listening to sermons or Scripture-based devotionals.
- Speaking the Word aloud over your life.

The more the Word gets in you, the less room sin has to grow.

The Love of His Word

When I read the Word, it's like I'm connecting directly with God. Every time I open my Bible, I'm not just reading words on a page—I'm spending time with my Father. I'm reading His heart, His thoughts, and His instructions. The Bible isn't just a book to me anymore—it's the living, breathing blueprint for how to walk with Him.

When I sit with the Word, I can literally feel His presence. There are moments when I'll open my Bible, not knowing exactly where to go, and God will lead me right to the passage that speaks to what I'm facing. It's like He's talking to me personally through every verse. That's what His Word does—it speaks life.

I have to be honest, though. When I first started reading the Bible, I didn't always understand it, especially the King James Version. The language felt heavy, and I struggled to make sense of what I was reading. So, I prayed. I asked God to open my understanding—to help me comprehend His Word and apply it to my life. And just like that, He did.

Now, when I read, the Holy Spirit teaches me. The Scriptures make sense, not because I'm smarter, but because God's Spirit gives me revelation. Sometimes, I'll use other versions to get clarity, but I always go back to prayer—because true understanding comes from Him.

What I love most about reading the Word is how it changes me. It softens me. It helps me to forgive. It humbles me. It gives me peace, even when everything around me is loud and chaotic. It keeps me anchored.

The more I read, the more I understand who God is—and the more I understand who I am in Him. Because when Christ lives in me, sin can't. The Word fills every empty place where sin used to live. It leaves no room for compromise. That's why I keep feeding on it. It's my daily bread.

Reading His Word has made me more confident—not in myself, but in Him. It's made me bold to share my story and to speak truth with love. It's helped me walk out the fruits of the Spirit: love, joy, peace, patience, kindness, goodness, faithfulness, gentleness, and self-control.

Because when your heart is full of the Word, temptation loses its voice.

Scripture Reflections

"Your word is a lamp to my feet and a light to my path." — Psalm 119:105
"The Word of God is living and active, sharper than any double-edged sword." — Hebrews 4:12
"Let the word of Christ dwell in you richly." — Colossians 3:16
"Man shall not live by bread alone, but by every word that proceeds out of the mouth of God." — Matthew 4:4

Reflection Thought:

When you fill yourself with the Word, you won't be ruled by the world. The Bible doesn't just change your thoughts—it transforms your entire life.

Get The Right Accountability Partner

Deliverance without accountability is an open door to relapse.

You need someone who:

- Prays with you and for you.
- Will tell you the truth, not just pat you on the back.
- Will check on your spirit, not just your schedule.
- Lives holy and is spiritually mature.
- Has no secret competition or hidden agenda.

Proverbs 27:17 (KJV) "Iron sharpeneth iron; so a man sharpeneth the countenance of his friend."

Pray that God will reveal or send your accountability partner. Not everyone is assigned to walk with you in spiritual maintenance.

If you're married, let your spouse be a spiritual partner. And if you're single, pray for God to assign a spiritually sound sister in Christ — not just a church friend.

Being Spiritually Accountable

When I talk about a spiritually sound sister, I'm really talking about an accountability partner. Someone God has assigned, not someone you've simply selected. Because when you're in a vulnerable place, still healing, still learning to walk in your new identity, you can't afford to be connected to just anyone.

Having an accountability partner is vital to your spiritual growth and deliverance. But before you choose one, you must pray. Ask God to send you a person who's spiritually mature, trustworthy, and able to handle your transparency with wisdom and grace. Someone who won't gossip about your pain but will guard your process.

Your accountability partner should be someone who knows how to pull your coat when you're slipping. Someone who can lovingly say, "Hey sis, remember what God brought you out of," or "Let's pray about this before you make a move." This isn't a friend who judges or condemns you; this is someone who's strong enough to intercede for you, pray with you, and remind you of what God said when your flesh wants to forget.

I had two accountability partners who were women that I trusted completely. One was a relative, and the other felt like one. Both were safe places for me to vent, cry, laugh, and talk through the real struggles of letting go. They didn't just listen—they redirected me. If I wanted to pick up the phone and call the wrong person, they were the ones I'd call instead. Sometimes we'd go get something to eat, talk about the Word, or just sit and let me breathe.

That's what accountability does—it gives you a chance to exhale. It reminds you that you're not alone, even when you feel like you are. It helps silence the enemy's lies that say you've lost something by walking away from what wasn't God's will.

Both of my accountability partners were godly women who spoke life over me. They never tore me down. They reminded me that I didn't lose anything when I walked away from sin—I gained everything.

But I'll say this again: be careful who you choose. Everyone who smiles in your face can't handle your story. Don't choose someone out of loneliness or vulnerability. Ask God to show you who's equipped to walk with you through the process without judging you or secretly rejoicing in your pain. The wrong accountability partner can lead you right back into the very thing you're trying to escape.

When God sends the right accountability partner, you'll know. She'll pray before she speaks. She'll point you to the Word, not her opinion. She'll help you grow—not just emotionally, but spiritually.

Scripture Reflections

"As iron sharpens iron, so one person sharpens another." — Proverbs 27:17

"Two are better than one, because they have a good return for their labor. If either of them falls down, one can help the other up." — Ecclesiastes 4:9–10

"Confess your faults one to another, and pray for one another, that ye may be healed." — James 5:16

Reflection Thought:

Accountability isn't control—it's covering. The right accountability partner doesn't chain you; she helps you stay free.

Discernment Is Protection

Sometimes relapses don't start with action — it starts with the feeling.

- That text message you shouldn't answer.
- That memory you begin to fantasize about.
- That outfit you wear when you want to attract the wrong attention.
- That show or song that awakens something God already buried.

It may seem small, but the Holy Spirit will warn you.

Warning Sent

I remember one particular day when I was cleaning out my closet. I have a tendency to hold onto clothes, especially the ones I think I might wear again. But this time, as I was going through my things, I came across an old outfit—one I used to wear when I was living as a side piece.

The moment I laid eyes on it, something in my spirit shifted. The Holy Spirit gave me this deep, uneasy feeling in my stomach. It wasn't just nostalgia—it was conviction. I knew right then that this wasn't just a piece of clothing anymore; it was a reminder of who I used to be and where I had been.

As nice as that outfit was, I knew I couldn't keep it. I couldn't justify holding onto something tied to such a painful and sinful part of my past. The Holy Spirit whispered, "All things are new." And when He said that, I knew what I had to do.

I took that outfit, put it in a bag, tied it up tight, and threw it not just in my indoor trash, but outside—completely away from my home. I didn't even want it lingering in my house, not even in the garbage can inside. That act may have seemed small, but it was deeply spiritual. It was symbolic of me removing what was old so that the new could stay.

Sometimes deliverance requires cleaning house. Literally. You can't hold onto things that represent who you used to be while asking God to mold you into someone new. There are objects, clothes, letters, pictures, even music, that carry spiritual residue from your past. If it reminds you of a sinful place or stirs old feelings that God delivered you from, it's time to release it.

When you clean your home, you're not just organizing your physical space—you're clearing your spiritual atmosphere. And when you've done that, anoint your home. Pray over every room. Declare peace, holiness, and newness over your space. Let the devil know that he no longer has a hiding place in your house, in your memories, or in your heart.

That day, when I threw that outfit away, I felt lighter. I felt peace. It was as if God said, "That chapter is over, and that outfit doesn't fit you anymore—because it belongs to who you used to be."

Scripture Reflections

"Therefore, if anyone is in Christ, he is a new creature: old things are passed away; behold, all things are become new." —2 Corinthians 5:17

"Let us throw off everything that hinders and the sin that so easily entangles." — Hebrews 12:1

"Create in me a clean heart, O God; and renew a right spirit within me." — Psalm 51:10

Reflection Thought:

Deliverance isn't always dramatic—it's daily obedience. Sometimes the holiest thing you can do is take out the trash.

1 Corinthians 10:13 (NIV)

"But when you are tempted, He will also provide a way out so that you can endure it."

God doesn't just forgive sin. He tries to help you avoid it.

If you ignore those nudges, that "something feels off" moment, you are walking willingly back into the very thing you prayed for God to free you from.

Stay Full So You're Not Vulnerable

The key to staying out of sin is staying filled with the Spirit.

You relapse when you are spiritually empty and emotionally vulnerable.
This is why you must:

- Stay in prayer.
- Fast regularly (not just when you're in crisis).
- Be honest when you're weak.
- Stay connected to your faith community.
- Protect your eyes, ears, and emotions.

The goal is not just to resist — it's to renew daily.

The Daily Renewal

Renewing daily means making a conscious choice every morning to invite God into every part of your day. When I wake up, the first thing I do before my feet even hit the floor is thank Him for waking me up. I thank Him for His grace and His mercy, because the fact that I'm alive means He's given me another chance to get it right.

Before I start my day, I pray. I ask Him to cover me, my children, my husband, my family, my church family, my community, my mother, and my siblings. I pray for His protection and His guidance. I ask Him to order my steps and to allow me to walk in His will and not my own.

Those prayers help me stay grounded. They prepare my heart and my mind for whatever the day may bring. Because let's be honest—life doesn't stop testing us just because we've been delivered. There are moments when people or situations will try your patience. There are times when anger rises up, when you want to respond in the flesh, when your emotions start to pull you backward.

And yes, there have been times when I've slipped—when frustration or irritation got the best of me. But even then, the Holy Spirit convicts me immediately. He doesn't let me rest in that space. I feel it in my spirit, and I have to stop and repent right then and there. That's what daily renewal looks like—it's allowing God to check you, correct you, and restore you in the moment.

It's waking up every day, understanding that I'm not perfect, but I'm covered. That I'm not flawless, but I'm forgiven. Renewal is not about staying spotless; it's about staying surrendered.

Part of my renewal process also means protecting my gates—my eyes, my ears, my emotions. I have to be careful about what I watch, what I listen to, and who I allow to speak into my life. I stay connected to my faith community because I know isolation is where the enemy works hardest. When I'm surrounded by prayer, worship, and the Word, I'm less likely to drift.

I also fast when the Lord leads me to—and sometimes even when He doesn't, because fasting helps keep my spirit sharp and my flesh in check. It's not about starving myself; it's about feeding my spirit.

Do I still make mistakes? Absolutely. But I no longer make the same ones I used to. I don't live the same life I once did. God has changed my heart, my mind, my desires, and my habits. He's given me the strength to be the woman, wife, and mother He called me to be.

Every day I renew my mind, and every day He renews my strength.

Scripture Reflections

"Because of the Lord's great love we are not consumed, for his compassions never fail. They are new every morning; great is your faithfulness." — Lamentations 3:22–23
"Be transformed by the renewing of your mind." — Romans 12:2
"Create in me a clean heart, O God, and renew a right spirit within me." — Psalm 51:10
"Those who wait upon the Lord shall renew their strength." — Isaiah 40:31

Reflection Thought:

Daily renewal isn't about perfection—it's about persistence. Every morning that you rise and say "Yes, Lord," He restores what the world tried to drain the day before.

Reflection of Chapter Nine:

The enemy doesn't mind your freedom. He fears your discipline.
Don't just get free — stay free.
Don't return to a place that God burned down for your good.

Declaration: Say This With Me

I will not go back.
I am free, and I am full.
My spirit rules over my flesh.
I crucify every ungodly craving.
I will fast and be strengthened.
I will pray and stay filled.
I will surround myself with truth and accountability.

I am not who I used to be.
I will not return to what God delivered me from.

Chapter Nine Prayer: A Prayer To Stay Free

Father God,

Thank You for my deliverance. Thank You for the grace that pulled me out. Now give me the strength to never return. Help me to recognize the traps, the familiar spirits, and the secret cravings that try to lead me back into bondage.

Teach me to fast with power. Help me to starve my flesh and feed my spirit. Fill me with Your Word. Saturate my soul with Your truth. Keep me hungry for righteousness and thirsty for You alone.

Send the right accountability partner into my life. Let them be bold, pure, and Spirit-filled. Surround me with voices that sharpen me and help me stay aligned.

I choose holiness. I choose freedom. I choose to stay in covenant. I will not go back.

In Jesus' name,
Amen.

Don't just cut the stem—pull the root. Freedom lasts when every door is shut and every desire is surrendered.

Chapter Ten: Glory After This

After everything I've shared, after the brokenness, the confusion, the shame, the side-piece days, the wandering, the rebellion, the pieces of myself that I gave away — there is still glory.

There is glory after this.

Glory after heartbreak.
Glory after loss.
Glory after sin.
Glory after repentance.
Glory after deliverance.

Romans 8:18 (KJV) "For I reckon that the sufferings of this present time are not worthy to be compared with the glory which shall be revealed in us."

I am living proof that God can redeem any story.

Freedom in Today!

Today, I feel free—completely and utterly free. I feel light in my spirit, unbound, unchained, and unashamed. There's no guilt, no heaviness, no weight from my past hanging over me anymore. The woman I once was is gone, and in her place stands a woman made whole, a woman restored by the grace of God.

When I look back on my past, I don't feel any ill feelings or sadness. I don't feel regret. I don't feel pain. I feel peace. I feel thankful. I feel humbled. Because the same God who could have left me in my brokenness chose instead to lift me up, dust me off, and call me His own.

I no longer carry the burden of shame. I no longer walk around trying to hide what God has already forgiven. Instead, I walk with confidence—not in myself, but in God's grace. I feel redeemed. I feel safe. I feel spiritually covered and protected because I know that He is with me.

And this isn't just a feeling—it's a knowing.
I know that I know that I know that God is with me. His Spirit lives within me. His peace surrounds me. His grace sustains me. That's the kind of assurance that only comes when you've truly been delivered and set free.

I don't take His grace lightly. Every day I thank Him for His mercy, for never leaving me, for loving me through my transformation. And because of His love, I can finally breathe again.

Living in Purpose After Deliverance

Choosing God wasn't just the best decision I ever made — it was the only decision that made me truly live.

I still remember the day I finally surrendered everything to Him. It was a day of spiritual refreshing. I decided to give my life over to God because deep down, I knew He was the only One who could fix what was broken, restore what was lost, and repair my life in a way that would bring Him glory. I wanted to live my life in a way that, when my time on earth is done, I would know without a shadow of a doubt that I would spend eternity with Him.

That day, I felt something shift within me. There was a peace that settled over my spirit—an indescribable calm that let me know I was right where I was meant to be. I wasn't worried anymore about who would love me or whether I would ever find happiness again, because I already had peace. The things that used to weigh on me, the worries and fears that once stole my joy, no longer had power.

When I surrendered, I also learned that God would still allow me to love again—but this time, to love the way He designed love to be: pure, holy, and whole.

And the most beautiful part of it all was realizing that everything I thought I wanted before didn't compare to what He wanted for me. My desires began to change. My will began to line up with His will. And when that happens—when your desires become what God desires for you—everything starts to align in perfect order.

That's when I truly began to live.

I'm no longer just existing.
I'm living in purpose.

- I get to wake up with peace.
- I get to walk in covenant.
- I get to speak with authority.
- I get to live in the light of truth.
- I get to love and be loved — God's way.

Deliverance was never the end.
It was the beginning.

The beginning of a life surrendered.
The beginning of a daily walk in holiness.
The beginning of my real identity.

Freedom Feels Like This

There is no peace like the peace that comes after repentance.
There is no love like the love that God pours out on His children who return to Him.

John 8:36 (KJV) "If the Son therefore shall make you free, ye shall be free indeed."

There is no more pretending. No more covering.
Just freedom.

When you truly surrender, you don't just break off chains — you put on new garments.

For me, those new garments feel spiritually light. It's as though the weight I once carried was traded for a robe of peace, grace, and victory. When I surrendered my life to God, I realized I had entered a win-win situation. I'm winning here on earth because Christ lives within me, and when I leave this earth, I'll keep on winning because I'll live with Him for eternity.

That's what it means when the chains fall off — you're not just free, you're clothed in victory. Every piece of shame, guilt, and pain is replaced with the garments of joy, peace, and purpose.

The victory was and is already mine — I just had to meet victory where it was waiting for me.

You wear peace.
You wear grace.
You wear purpose.
You wear glory.

His Grace and Mercy Found Me

I'm not perfect.
I never claimed to be.

I still get tempted.
I still have to fight my flesh.
I still have to wake up every day and choose to live holy.
But I no longer live in bondage.

Because His grace and mercy found me, pulled me out, cleaned me up, and filled me with purpose.

Lamentations 3:22–23 (ESV) "The steadfast love of the Lord never ceases; His mercies never come to an end; they are new every morning..."

Every day is a gift.
Every moment is a mercy.

We are not promised tomorrow.
We are not promised the next hour.
But as long as we are still breathing, we have the opportunity to worship, surrender, and live holy.

God Deserves the Glory

I am only here because of Him.
This book only exists because He authored my deliverance.

I didn't write this because I have all the answers.
I wrote this because I know what it means to be broken and made whole.

When you put God first —
Before relationships.
Before desires.
Before careers.
Before anything —
He puts everything else into divine order.

Matthew 6:33 (KJV) "But seek ye first the kingdom of God, and his righteousness; and all these things shall be added unto you."

Put Him first, and let everything else fall in place.

First Place Always

When I put God first in my life, everything fell into place according to His will.

Allowing Him to be first means giving Him full control — not just of my spirit, but of my household, my marriage, my family, and every area that concerns me. When I handle God's work first — when I give Him my time, my attention, and my obedience — He takes care of everything else.

He provides for my household. He covers my family. He ensures that my needs are met — the food on my table, the clothes on my back, the peace in my home. Everything falls into its rightful, divine order when God is at the head.

With God as the head of my life, my husband as the head of our home, and our family following the order He established, there's peace. There's balance. There's stability. That's the divine structure that keeps our home blessed.

When I put Him first, things begin to flow — spiritually, emotionally, financially, and mentally. God has a way of blessing not just my home, but everything I put my hands to. And the best part is knowing that when doors close, I don't have to worry or force them back open, because I trust the One who holds the keys.

Putting Him first means trusting Him completely — with my life, my purpose, and my future.

A Final Word to You, My Reader

If you're reading this right now, I want you to know this truth:
You are loved.

Not because of who you are — but because of who God is.

You don't have to carry the shame.
You don't have to keep pretending.
You don't have to stay broken, bitter, hidden, or halfway holy.

God is waiting for you — just like the father in the story of the prodigal son.

He's not looking at your past.
He's looking at your heart.
And He's saying: "Come home."

If You're Ready to Come Home – Say This Prayer:

Heavenly Father,

I thank You for loving me even when I was far from You.
I acknowledge that I have sinned, and I've lived in ways that did not honor You.
But today, I repent. I turn from my sins. I surrender my will and my desires to You.
I believe in my heart that Jesus is Lord, and I confess it with my mouth.
I believe that He died for my sins and rose from the grave so that I could be free.
Lord, come into my heart. Clean me. Restore me.
Fill me with Your Spirit and teach me how to live for You.
Today, I declare that I am Yours.
In Jesus' name,
Amen.

Reflection of Chapter Ten:

Deliverance is not the end of your story — it's the beginning of God's glory in your life.

Declaration: Say This With Me

I am delivered.
I am free.
I am healed.
I am chosen.
I am walking in purpose.
I will never go back.
I am a covenant keeper.
I am God's daughter.
And there is glory — after this.

May The Lord Bless You

Thank you for taking this journey with me.

May this book be a mirror, a weapon, and a reminder of who you are and whose you are.
May you rise in power, walk in holiness, and live with boldness.

You are not a side piece.
You are not just a piece.
You are God's masterpiece.

Walk in covenant.
Live in truth.
And never forget — there is GLORY after this.

Amen.

From Brokenness to Glory

As I look back over my journey, I no longer see shame, the pain, or the mistakes; I see the grace of God. Every broken piece that once caused me sorrow has become a reflection of God's mercy. What the enemy meant for destruction, God used for deliverance. What once silenced me now gives me a voice. And what once felt like death became the birthplace of new life in Christ.

I am living proof that God can take the most shattered vessel and make it whole again. I am not defined by who I was, but by who He called me to be. My past no longer imprisons me—it propels me. And now, I walk in freedom, clothed in grace, covered in His glory, and standing as a witness that there is no story too broken for God to redeem.

Prayers For Every Reader

Heavenly Father,

I thank You for every heart that has opened these pages and walked through this journey with me. Lord, I ask that You bless each reader who has finished this book. Let them not only see my testimony but recognize the power of Your hand in their own story. May every word written here stir something deeper—a hunger for truth, healing, and freedom that only You can give.

Father, for those who have stumbled and want to return home, I ask that You meet them right where they are. For those who have never known You but feel Your tug on their hearts, I ask that You draw them closer now.

If that's you, whether you've never given your life to Christ or you want to rededicate your life to Him, you can pray this prayer:

Lord Jesus, I come to You just as I am. I confess that I am a sinner in need of Your grace. I believe that You died for my sins and rose again, and today I ask You to come into my heart and be my Lord and Savior. Forgive me of my sins, cleanse me, and make me new. I surrender my life to You completely. Teach me how to walk in Your will and live by Your Word.

Thank You for forgiving me, for saving me, and for welcoming me home.
In Jesus' name,
Amen.

Father, I thank You for every soul who just prayed that prayer. Seal them with Your love and fill them with Your Spirit. Let peace overflow in their hearts, healing flow through their minds, and purpose awaken in their souls. Surround them with godly people, strengthen their faith daily, and remind them that their story is not over—it's just beginning.

Now may the Lord bless you and keep you.
May His face shine upon you and give you peace.
May His grace go before you; His mercy follow you, and His love forever surround you.
You are free. You are loved. You are whole.

In Jesus' name,
Amen.

Acknowledgements

I would first like to acknowledge my husband, Bishop Owens F. Shepard. Thank you for being my covering, my protector, my encourager, and the man God placed in my life to help push me toward my purpose. Your drive, your strength, and your unwavering belief in me have motivated me to do my very best. Thank you for never allowing me to settle, for reminding me of the God-given assignments in my life, and for pushing me to walk fully in them. I love you deeply and appreciate you more than words could ever express.

To all of our children, thank you for being my daily motivation. You give me the drive to keep going, to keep growing, and to strive to be better. Because of all of you, I desire to be a better mother, a better person, and a living example of what it means to be a God-fearing woman. Everything I do is with the hope that you see Christ in me and are encouraged to walk boldly in who God has called you to be.

To my writing coach, Ebony Nicole Smith, I am forever grateful. Thank you for partnering with me on this journey and for helping pull everything out of me that needed to be on these pages. You knew the right questions to ask and the right words to draw out of me. You could draw out the depth, the truth, and the "meat" of this book when I didn't always know how to do it myself. Because of your guidance, I was able to give my complete attention to this project. You were truly one of the key people God used in bringing this book to life, and I am thankful for the opportunity to continue working with you, Lord willing.

I would also like to acknowledge my family, my mother, my siblings, my cousins, my nieces and nephews, my aunts and uncles, and my family near and far. I am grateful to be connected to you and honored to be a part of the family God chose for me. When I look at my family, I see strength, resilience, growth, and legacy. Each of us strives to live well, and I am thankful for the lessons, the love, and the foundation that have shaped who I am today.

A very special acknowledgment goes to my mother, the matriarch of our family. She is a strong woman of faith, a woman of God, and an example of perseverance and grace. I adore her, I honor her, and I love her deeply. Much of who I am today is rooted in what I have learned from her and from the family legacy she continues to uphold.

To my friends, my close friends who are more than friends and have become sisters and brothers to me, thank you. God allowed our paths to cross, allowed us to pour into one another, and allowed genuine bonds to be formed. Thank you for showing up, for supporting me, for praying for me, and for standing with me in every season. Whether you have been in my life since childhood or entered later along the journey, you know who you are. I thank God for each of you and for the circle He has placed around me.

To my church family and church community, I want to sincerely thank you from the depths of my heart. I am truly grateful that God saw fit to connect our lives together for such a time as this. The love, support, encouragement, and godliness that dwell within our church family are gifts that I never take for granted.

I thank God for the unity we share, for the prayers we pray for one another, and for the way we stand beside each other through every season of life. I am grateful that we are more than just a congregation; we are family. We motivate one another, uplift one another, and labor together in ministry both inside and outside the four walls of the church.

One of the greatest blessings in my life has been being connected to a body of believers who truly love God and genuinely love people. I appreciate the servants of God at God Healing Temple who continue to serve faithfully, minister wholeheartedly, and walk together in unity and purpose. I would also like to extend my heartfelt gratitude to the many servants of God, ministries, pastors, leaders, and church communities who have connected with our ministry throughout the years.

Thank you to those who have poured into God Healing Temple with love, wisdom, prayer, encouragement, and support. Kingdom work is never done alone, and I am grateful for every divine connection, every act of fellowship, and every relationship God has allowed us to build within the body of Christ. It is a blessing to be connected to a community of believers who continue to strengthen, uplift, and encourage one another in love and unity. I am forever grateful for each person God has placed in my church family and church community. Your presence in my life has been a blessing, and I honor the bond that God has allowed us to share.

I am grateful for every relationship, every connection, and every person God has used to encourage, strengthen, and support me along the way. This book is not mine alone; it is the result of love, family, friendship, faith, prayer, and obedience.

For all of this, I am truly thankful.

In Memory Of

My father was a firm man, a true disciplinarian. He believed deeply in structure, correction, and accountability. He understood discipline in its fullest sense and believed in the principle of the rod, just as Scripture teaches: "Spare the rod, spoil the child." He did not believe in sparing the rod by any means, and he stood unwaveringly in that conviction.

Through his firmness and discipline, lessons were planted about responsibility, consequences, and the strength of character. Though his methods were tough, they played a role in shaping the resilience and determination that live within me today.

Though he is no longer here, his influence remains. I carry his lessons, his strength, and his legacy with me.

I pray that if he were able to see me now, he would be proud, not only of this book, but of the woman of God I have become.

You are remembered.
You are honored.
Your legacy lives on.

In Loving Memory of Elder Eric Floyd

In loving memory of Elder Eric Floyd, whose passing was both sudden and untimely, I pause to reflect on the profound impact he had on my life and the lives of so many others in our church. I remember clearly the moment he spoke a prophetic word over me, declaring that the Lord would use me mightily-that I would be a vessel for God, that the books placed within me would come forth, and that my voice would grow stronger in the Lord.

Those words have never left me. They continue to echo in my spirit, especially now, as I witness the unfolding of God's promises in my life.

Although his time with us was shorter than we desired, I am grateful for the legacy he left behind. He was a pillar within our church and church community-someone who led with humility, strength, and a genuine heart for God's people. He was not only a servant in ministry, but also an example to follow.

Today, I honor his memory with gratitude. I believe that if he were here, he would be smiling, seeing the very prophetic word God spoke through him coming to pass. His life, though brief, was impactful, meaningful, and rooted in God.

His legacy lives on-not only in memory, but in the fruit of the lives he touched.

ABOUT THE AUTHOR

Lakisha Shepard is a woman of faith, strength, and purpose whose life journey reflects grace, transformation, and divine timing. A devoted servant of God first and foremost, she walks boldly in the call placed upon her life to inspire, uplift, and help others discover healing through truth and faith.

A retired Deputy Sheriff Jailer and now Community Engagement Manager and Supervisor at Enterprise Security Consulting and Training, Inc., Lakisha continues to serve her community with compassion and conviction. She is a devoted wife to Bishop Owens F. Shepard and a loving mother devoted to their children, finding joy and balance in both ministry and family.

Lakisha is the author of Side Piece is the New Concubine, her debut work that marks the beginning of many visions being brought to life. With other projects and ventures in the making, she stands in this season of becoming, where purpose meets preparation, and the visions God has entrusted to her begin to manifest. This is her first book, but certainly not her last.

To God Be All The Glory

This book is first and foremost dedicated to You, Lord. Before there was a story, before there was pain, before there was healing, there was You.

I dedicate every page, every tear, every lesson, and every victory back to You. Because if it had not been for You, Your grace, Your mercy, and Your covering, I would not be here to tell this story.

You saw me when I was broken. You kept me when I didn't even know how to keep myself. You loved me through decisions, through seasons, and through places that I am not proud of, but You never left me there.

This book is my "yes" to You.
My surrender.
My testimony.
My offering.

Let every word bring You glory.
Let every reader feel Your presence.
Let every woman who reads this know that there is still redemption, healing, and purpose in You.

I am because You are.

With all that I am, I give this book back to You.

Your Daughter,
Lakisha Shepard